862-709
ONE

/O

A Plac

Caring

by Tom O'Neill

Printed and Published 2000 by
EDUCATIONAL PRINTING SERVICES LTD.
Albion Mill, Water Street, Blackburn, BB6 7QR.
Telephone: 01254 882080   Fax: 01254 882010
web site: www.eprint.co.uk

Editor's Preface

In the summer of 1979 I was giving a tutorial at Exeter University with one of the students on our social work course, Richard Airley, who had been in residential child care work before coming to Exeter. In talking about his work he mentioned that he had modelled his approach on that of Tom O'Neill. Seeing that I did not recognize the name, he went on to tell me that he had worked with Tom in Sussex; that Tom was Dennis O'Neill's brother; and that he had been in residential work with children for many years.

While he was telling me these facts Richard must have seen many changes of expression on my face, registering some of the amazement, excitement and wonder I was feeling. Dennis O'Neill's death at the hands of his foster-father in 1945 was in many ways comparable with Maria Colwell's death in 1973. The tragedy had led to a public outcry and major reforms of services for deprived children - a whole new service, in fact. There was something of the child's story-book in the notion of Dennis's brother working in that service, helping to give a better deal to the next generation of children in need. I found myself profoundly affected by the picture of someone so close to a classic victim subsequently devoting his life to the protection of other vulnerable children.

My excitement increased when Richard told me that Tom was writing a book about his life and work. I could scarcely wait to tell my colleague and co-editor, Jean Packman, of the news. As I expected (for she had worked in the child care service for many years), she was equally moved and equally keen to meet Tom and see his book. Richard warned me that Tom was a modest and retiring person but agreed to put us in touch.

A couple of months later I met Tom in London, where Richard was doing a placement. He is small in stature, wiry and fit-looking; he has very twinkling eyes and a long, wavy smile. Although he must now be in his early fifties, it takes no effort of the imagination to see him as a mischievous boy of fourteen. For a while we joined in the office chatter; one of the social workers was describing how the mother of a child in care habitually boiled pages of the Bible and drank a distillation of the ink from them. Tom remarked that this must be what was meant by thirsting after righteousness.

This book is partly an account of Tom's remarkable life, and it faithfully reflects his personality and his experiences. When Dennis was removed from home and fostered, Tom, who was several years older, was in an approved school. By the time Dennis was killed, Tom had started on the long road away from delinquency and despair. Until he was seventeen he had met little better than indifference and routine responses from the officials he came across in schools and courts; he also encountered much worse - callousness, vindictiveness and dishonesty. Then, suddenly, he experienced real caring, forgiveness and hope. His life was transformed. But it was many years before he was able to integrate his early experiences with what he had become. Tom was in his forties before he talked about the tragedy with his brother Terry, who was with Dennis in the foster home. His decision to write about it arose from a journey they made together back to Bank Farm, Hope Valley - which provides the book's title.

I feel privileged to have been involved in the publication of this unique book. Sadly, there have been other child care tragedies since Dennis O'Neill, and there will be more; but it is very unlikely that any other tragedy will have such an ideal sequel. Tom O'Neill's story is the perfect answer to those cynics and pessimists who doubt the value of offering whole-hearted and unconditional help to deprived and delinquent children. It also explodes determinist myths about the consequences of growing up in poor and problematic families. But, above all, Tom O'Neill can provide inspiration for a new generation of child care workers and a message of hope for a new generation of children.   BILL JORDAN

Contents

I would like to dedicate this book to my wife, Gwyn, and my two sons, Bernard and Philip, in appreciation of their help and encouragement, but particularly for their understanding over the years.

Introduction

Dennis O'Neill is beaten to death.
IT MUST NEVER HAPPEN AGAIN.
Maria Colwell is beaten to death.
IT MUST NEVER HAPPEN AGAIN.

Two children died. There were twenty-eight years between the two deaths, but can we learn the lesson now so that it will not happen again?

I first decided to write this book in the hope that I could help in some way to prevent a repeat of what happened in 1945.

On 9 January 1945 my brother, Dennis O'Neill, was beaten to death by his foster-father in a lonely farmhouse in Shropshire. Twenty-eight years later, on 6 January 1973, Maria Colwell was beaten to death by her step-father in a council house in Brighton. Both deaths resulted in a public outcry about the standards of official supervision of the children. In many respects, if I write about one child, I write about both.

In both instances there appeared to be a serious shortage of staff, which meant that the people responsible for the children's supervision were so severely handicapped that they were unable to carry out their duties effectively. Geographically, there were difficulties. Maria was being supervised by the East Sussex County Council, while she was living in an area which would normally have been supervised by a Brighton social worker. Dennis was living in Hope Valley, in Shropshire, but was in the care of the Newport (Monmouthshire) Education Committee. There were conflicting reports. One worker would report that he was not satisfied with the situation; another worker from a different agency would report that it appeared that things were settling down nicely.

Absences from school were not satisfactorily followed up, although it was reported that both children were working as drudges during the time that they were supposed to be attending school. It was said that Maria was well-drilled with visitors. She knew what she had to say. Dennis was also trained from a very early age to say the right things. Neither child had the opportunity to be alone with a visiting officer. In neither case could a visiting officer really see the conditions in which the children were living.

These similarities are very disturbing in themselves, but there are even more alarming parallels. The children suffered terribly for prolonged periods before their deaths, both from the conditions in which they lived and from the treatment they were given, yet throughout these periods they were being seen by officials. (It is possible that in the light of the suffering they endured beforehand their deaths were their escapes.) It is obvious from the evidence that much of their distress was *noticed*. In both cases it was stated quite categorically that there was a deterioration in the child's appearance. Maria was seen to have bruises, and she walked with a limp. Dennis was seen to have bruises and ulcerated and chafed legs, and he walked with a limp. They were both accused of lying. Maria's injuries were attributed to 'falling down', 'falling off a scooter'. Many of Dennis's injuries were supposed to have been caused while fighting with his brother.

It was winter. Maria was reported to be wearing inadequate clothing for the time of year. Her legs were too thin to enable her to keep her socks up. Dennis complained bitterly about the cold nights because his bed coverings were completely inadequate to keep out the cold.

One almost eerie similarity is the 'deferred' card, a bureaucratic procedure spanning twenty-eight years and hundreds of miles. A visitor to the farm at Shropshire sent an urgent message to the Newport Education Committee stating that it was a matter of *great urgency* that Dennis be visited. The person who would normally have dealt with this was away at the time. She was on leave - I am not certain whether it was annual leave or sick leave. However, the card was marked 'To await return' and then filed away. It was thought to be a matter of urgency that Maria should have a school medical examination. She did not keep her appointment. Her card was marked DNA ('Did not Attend') and put at the bottom of the pile.

Sometimes children in care seem to have almost too many medical inspections. They have medicals on admission, medicals at school and very easy access to the general practitioner. Often, within a few weeks of their last inspection by a doctor in the home, they are seen by the school doctor, who could well be the same person. It is nearly incredible that both Dennis and Maria should have received so little medical attention.

Although they were both already deprived, they were forbidden outings, treats and so on. Perhaps this came under the category of punishments. Perhaps it was considered that they were unworthy of treats, although others around them were not being similarly deprived. They were expected to watch others enjoying themselves.

Beatings, poor clothes, jobs to do, false accusations, no treats. All these things are terrible to think about. Yet to me one of the most awful aspects is that through all the period of beatings, humiliations, questions and suffering the children were being killed slowly, through starvation. At the time of her death Maria, whose stomach was empty, weighed a mere 36 pounds. Her breakfast was dry crusts. The other children were told to come in for their dinner, but there was none for her. She probably watched the others eating. At the time of his death Dennis, whose stomach showed no traces of food, weighed just over 4 stone at thirteen years of age. He sucked the cows' udders to get some sustenance. He was punished for stealing the cows' fodder or a swede. He stood, the night before he died, watching other people eat a meal.

I feel very close to both these children - to Dennis because he was my brother, but also to Maria because for sixteen years I worked with children in care. There are obvious links between my family background and the work I chose to do. Yet for many years I concealed my background and spoke to few people of it. To become a residential social worker with children I had to overcome a poor education and strong feelings of stigma - it never occurred to me to write about my early experiences until I had been doing this work for many years.

In 1970 an opportunity arose for me to get a post out of residential work but still working with children. When I applied I was asked to visit the children's officer, who told me, in a kindly way, that because I was untrained I would be at a disadvantage, so it would be better if I tried to get accepted for the basic training course in residential child care.

After some doubts I decided that I would apply. My first choice was the course at Cardiff. When I decided on Cardiff there were many things I took into consideration. First of all, knowing that initially I would have a struggle to cope with the academic side of the course, I decided that I should be far away from my place of work, so that I wouldn't have that worrying me. I was the superintendent of a fairly large children's home and was leaving my wife in the home with an acting superintendent. I knew there might be problems at the outset, and I didn't really feel that I could, or should, become involved in these. Secondly, I came from Newport, and as this is only twelve miles from Cardiff, I would have some contact with my family, which would help me over any loneliness or homesickness I might suffer. (In fact, I was going to stay with one of my brothers.)

In one way, I was aware that the course was *bound* to reveal my identity, wherever I studied, because Dennis's death was such an important event in the history of child care. His foster-father was charged with manslaughter and was sentenced to six years in prison. There was a great public outcry. A public inquiry was held, presided over by Sir Walter Monckton, KCMG, KCVO, MC, KC. A committee was set up

> to inquire into existing methods of providing for children who from loss
> of parents or from any cause whatever are deprived of a normal home
> life with their own parents or relatives; and to consider what further
> measures should be taken to ensure that these children are brought up

under conditions best calculated to compensate them for the lack of parental care*

under the chairmanship of Dame Myra Curtis, CBE. The Curtis Report was unsparing in its criticism of standards of care, and the 1948 Children Act came into being.

I was well aware that any course of this nature would deal with the 1948 Act. It was the whole basis of the system in which I now worked. It was at the interview in Cardiff, however, that it first really dawned on me how my own life and this piece of history were so painfully linked. The next part of my interview was sheer hell. I was asked for more details of my background; I perspired freely and felt that I would never get through the interview. I had to try to justify my career in terms of those distant events, explaining both how they had affected me and how I had grown and changed in the years since. I was highly sensitive to the reactions of these people, who knew my family, even though they had never seen me before, and who were now judging my suitability for the work to which I had given my life. I was very relieved when they told me soon afterwards that I was accepted.

So I started on the course, and it wasn't too long before the story of the O'Neill family came to the fore. It was awkward for me when I had to acknowledge to the other students that I was indeed a member of this family. It became a wonderful moment, though, because I was accepted for what I had become in spite of my early upbringing. As time went on and I began to speak more freely of my childhood and youth, I became more conscious of how my early years had shaped my feelings in adult life. As it became clearer that instead of being a millstone around my neck, my past experiences could be of help to others, my tutors suggested that I commit to paper the story I had to tell. There was a great deal of reluctance on my part initially, but then something happened that clarified my thinking; it also led to one of the most moving experiences of my life.

---

* *Report of the Care of Children Committee.* Cmnd. 6922, HMSO, 1946 (known as the Curtis Report).

Introduction

One of the students decided that he would do a project on fostering, and it was suggested that I may be able to help him to fill in the details of some aspects of fostering before 1948. I agreed to ask my brother Terry about this. He had spent a number of years in foster-homes and had been with Dennis when he died. We had never talked about this; as a matter of fact, we had never really talked about anything. On this particular occasion we talked for a little, and he offered to help if he could. This was the start. It led to an amazing and emotional breakthrough in our relationship, to communication about past events which had previously been too painful to touch upon, to long journeys, tears, reunions and happiness. I shall describe all this later in this book.

My tutor continued to encourage me to write my story, and I talked it over with Terry. We both agreed that this was a story that might do something to prevent the same things from happening again. We decided not to involve the other members of the family but just to tell our stories - the stories of two little boys, many years ago, whose paths went in different directions only to meet up again years later.

I cannot adequately thank the tutors and students on the course for all the help and encouragement they gave me during the time that I spent writing. It was a most emotional and difficult task at times, and I really must have been, on occasions, a burden to others. I thank them for their kindness and patience. Most of all, though, I thank them for their friendship.

TOM O'NEILL

1 Beautiful Days of Childhood

It was a frightening experience to stand before the magistrates in the courtroom. Not that this was the first time I had done so. I had been in this situation on quite a number of occasions previously. I had been fined on one occasion, placed on probation on another, and in some ways had ceased to be afraid of appearing before the magistrates.

This time, though, something had changed. It had nothing to do with the seriousness of the offence, which was rather a trivial one, really. In the company of others, I had stolen some empty lemonade bottles from a lorry. But somehow I felt that the outcome of this appearance in court was going to be different. I was frightened.

The evidence was given, and each of us was asked in turn if there was anything we would like to say to the court. This, incidentally, was the only time that *both* my parents were present in court. They too were asked if they would like to say anything. Of course, they intimated that I was really a good boy but had become mixed up with seedy characters who had led me astray.

After some discussion between the magistrates, it was time to pass sentence. There were about nine of us altogether, and one by one each boy was told what punishment he would receive. A fine here, probation there and so on, until I was the only one left to receive sentence. It appeared that the magistrates did not accept my parents' views; indeed, they even considered, because of my past misdemeanours, that I was the leader of this particular episode. I had been treated leniently enough in the past, and therefore they had no alternative but to send me to an approved school.

I had reason to be afraid. It was a terrible shock to hear those words, and I can remember having a hysterical outburst. I cried, I screamed, I kicked and I struggled, I pleaded to be allowed to go home, I swore that I would never get into any more trouble if only I was given one more chance. It was all to no avail. It didn't matter what I now promised, there was no going back on their decision as far as they were concerned. It was an approved school for me.

I should tell you my age at this time. It so happened that for some reason or other there had been a terrible confusion over our ages. At some time in their lives my two sisters and two of my brothers had had their ages reduced by two years. I cannot explain how or why this happened but can only state that this caused me some inconvenience right up until the time I was seventeen, when I was summoned to the Ministry of Labour offices at Pontypridd, Glamorgan, to explain why I had not registered for National Service when I had attained the age of seventeen and three-quarter years. I explained that I had only just reached the age of seventeen, but I was told that as far as they were concerned, I was now nineteen years of age. I was warned about the consequences of trying to evade registration and was given ten days to produce proof of my claim. I did so and since then have been able to produce a birth certificate when required. My sister, though, still has some difficulty in proving her age. At the time of my court appearance I was really eleven years old, though it was thought by all concerned that I was thirteen.

So at eleven I was regarded as a criminal and was treated as such, was taken away struggling and handcuffed to a policeman and transported from Newport to Cardiff in a 'Black Maria', the name that we gave to the police vans at that time.

What had happened to me in my eleven years that had brought me to this situation? What was it that had made me into a crook with a number of court appearances? Why was I, at eleven, suddenly taken away from my parents, brothers and sisters and home?

I do not find it easy to write about my family. My parents are dead, but some of my sisters and brothers still live in Newport, very near where we grew up. I have moved away, and perhaps because of the work I have done I reflect upon our early life in ways that are strange to them. I worry about causing them pain by what I write, and above all I want to avoid blaming anyone.

However, I feel that I should say something about my family and the conditions in which we lived. There are many aspects of my early life that I cannot recall with any accuracy. I have often been told about two members of the family of whom I know next to nothing. One was Thomas, who died before I was born; the other was Christine, who also died at a very early age and whom I can hardly remember.

My father, known as John, came from a large, respectable family of Irish origin. He was a short and stocky man, always good for a laugh and regarded as the life and soul of the party. He also had a violent temper, though, and when roused could be quite vicious and physically aggressive. He used to tell me that he was a blacksmith's striker by trade, but on my birth certificate he is described as a labourer. He served in the army in both world wars; in the second he was invalided out after Dunkirk. He was very tough and hard-hitting and was at one time, apparently, an army boxing champion. I can remember him explaining to me once the meaning of the phrase 'black sheep of the family'. He said that this was how his own family looked on him.

Of course, between the wars (and later), like so many others, he was unemployed for long periods of time, relying on the dole for the wherewithal to bring up the family. He was a heavy drinker and smoker; although we always seemed to be short of money in the house, he managed to buy his beer and cigarettes. For beer money - and free beer - he often took on a part-time job in a public house in Newport called the Robin Hood. There were periods when he had a job away from home. Then he used to come back at weekends and would have money to spend. These were the times that there would be treats for the family. It did not happen very often, so these treats were special occasions for us.

My mother's name was Mabel Blodwen. She came from a small family; she had one brother, and her mother was a widow long before I was born. She herself was born in Pontypridd. My grandmother was very strict and respectable and was upset by the way things had turned out for my mother. Mabel had been beautiful when she was young, I was told, but I knew her only as a pathetic, snuff-addicted woman, whose child-bearing and frequent beatings from my father had taken their toll. She was blind in one eye, which often had to be treated with an ointment, the effect of which was to make the eye appear to weep constantly. She also had a large goitre, which in her younger days she kept covered with a scarf.

I believe that my parents were married in 1918. Theirs was a stormy marriage, to say the least. There were many, many rows. Two words that I remember all too well from my childhood were 'whore' and 'whoremaster'. I had no idea what the words meant at first but made it my business to find out. I cannot say for certain whether either was unfaithful, but the innuendo was certainly prevalent.

The oldest member of my family whom I can remember was my brother Cyril. He was fostered by his maternal grandmother and remained with her until he got married. I can never remember him living at home; in fact, he used to call my mother by her Christian name, which, of course, in those days was not the custom. He apparently had an accident when he was young which left him with a peculiar gait when walking.

My sister Betty was the next oldest. She was the only member of the family to stay with my parents after all the others had left home. She is very interesting to talk to about the early days. She really believes that the authorities were to blame for everything and that there was nothing wrong with the family at all. She loved our mother and had a deep affection for our 'Dadda' though she sometimes had a tough time at his hands. She is a really rough diamond, but what a character she is! She has a heart of gold and is so fun-loving that she gets every ounce of satisfaction out of life that she can. Before my mother died she was in a virtual coma for a long time. Betty cared for her for all that time; words cannot describe the devotion that she gave her.

Then there was my brother Charles. I always felt that Charles had a little more class than the rest of us. For one thing, he appeared to be honest. I remember two incidents fairly clearly. One was when he found a parcel of clothing and brought it home saying that he ought to hand it in to the police. He was out-voted, although, as it happened, somebody had seen him pick it up and had reported it, so that we had a visit from the police anyway. The other incident involved my finding a purse containing £12. Actually, I saw the woman drop it, but as she was getting into a nice car anyway, she must have been very rich and would not have suffered any hardship because of the loss. However, it took all my powers of persuasion to convince Charles that there was no point in handing the money in to the police, and I finally said that she probably lived a long way away. We kept it. When the three youngest children were removed from home Charles went to live with friends. This was his own idea - he ran out of the house when the NSPCC inspector arrived to take the children away. He made his own way in life and never did return home.

I was the next in line and was followed by my sister Rosina. She is the loyal one of the family. She it is who has done everything possible to keep the family together, even though separated by many miles. She has tried to maintain the links where possible, remembering birthdays and sending cards. A 'jewel' in our family is Rose. I remember that as a child she used to suffer from fits of some kind. The answer in our house was to throw her on to the bed in a very rough manner to bring her out of them. This seemed to be very effective. She spent many hours while in bed, singing at the top of her voice and shaking her head from side to side. Rose had a very sad life at the start of our separation. I think that the splitting up of the family caused her more heartbreak than any other member of the family. Somehow, I don't think that she has ever really got over the whole affair. Her sadness goes very deep.

Of the three younger brothers who followed I remember very little. These were Dennis, Terrence and Frederick. I remember that Dennis had pneumonia as a child and came very close to dying. (I was under the impression at the time that this was caused by eating coloured sweets that had the appearance of real fruits.) Dennis was a very quiet lad. I recall that he had very badly discoloured teeth. Terry was the tough guy of the three. He had far more about him than Dennis and was more of a leader. Fred was the really shy one. Of course, he was extremely young when taken away from home.

These, then, were the members of our family. By the time I was born we had already become something of a problem family. My father had been imprisoned in 1923, when he served a month for the ill treatment of his oldest child (I believe this to have been Cyril, but none of us seems to know for a fact, as nobody in the family can positively state which of us is the oldest). In 1939 he was to be imprisoned again, this time with my mother, and the children were taken away from home for a month, as I shall explain later.

We were extremely poor. My mother had her ways of obtaining food and money. First, there was the pawn shop. She used this method quite frequently. She would take articles to the local pawnbroker and would receive in exchange cash which was lent at a weekly interest rate of about twopence. The most 'pawnable' items were a suit belonging to my father and my mother's wedding ring. The suit was a useful article because it was rarely worn. Pawned on Monday, redeemed on Friday, pawned on Monday and so on. As for food and cigarettes, my mother bought those 'on tick' from the local shop. Here again it was a case of 'have now, pay later'. The strange thing to me was that having paid the bill in part, we would immediately buy more on tick. Although she was a poor manager, my mother could nevertheless produce a very appetizing stew from all sorts of odds and ends. Scraps were sometimes available from the butcher, and a few vegetables gathered from the floor of the greengrocer's went a long way. In those days we also used to have 'sop' to eat (this consisted of bread soaked in milk), and my mother made us condensed milk sandwiches. On top of this, of course, we were given free milk and free dinners at school. All in all, I suppose, we did very well.

Housing and education were always problems to us - problems that went hand in hand. We moved home regularly, and we often had to change schools because of that. Looking back, I can remember seventeen houses we lived in before I was eleven. There may even have been others which I do not recall. We always seemed to be on the move, often late at night. To us the phrase 'moonlight flit' was very real. We used some strange methods of transport to carry our few pitiful belongings from one house to another. On one occasion I remember pushing a pram absolutely loaded with bits and pieces. Another time we borrowed a handcart from somewhere to move our goods. We didn't really wonder why we had to keep on the move. To us it was a fact of life. Landlords were dissatisfied with the way we looked after the houses we were living in. The rent was usually well overdue, and there was no money with which to pay. Sometimes the electricity or gas was cut off, or both, and we were left without warmth except for the pieces of household fittings which we broke up and used as firewood. And so on. Whatever the reasons for moving, the outcome was the same. Another house, another district, another school.

The area of Newport in which we lived mostly was Pillgwenlly, known to all and sundry as 'Pill'. It is Newport's dockland; many of the streets are narrow and dirty, and a large number of families lived in complete squalor. We were certainly in that category. Our house was usually filthy, our clothes shabby and unkempt. Our bodies were generally covered in rashes and fleabites. Bedding was anything that we could reasonably use - often our overcoats (if we owned any) were put on top of the bed at night. I really don't remember how many we slept to the bed.

I went to so many schools in Newport and was so unhappy at all but one of them that it became comparatively easy to justify playing truant. The reason why I was so unhappy was because I was different from many of the other children. My clothes were dirty and torn; often they were handouts or articles which we had picked up somewhere. Whenever I had a haircut the operation was performed by my father, who always left prominent 'steps' in the back of my hair, much to the amusement of the other kids. My boots often came to me courtesy of the Education Committee and were stamped to that effect so that there could be no possibility of pawning them. To cap it all, I was, as I have said, usually covered with a rash. It was plain for all to see that this was a result of the way we lived. When I was in school the teachers had no difficulty in finding me a place to sit: invariably, it was at the back of the class.

At all the schools I attended there was only one teacher who, to my mind, treated me with any consideration whatsoever. She was the only one for whom I did any work of a worthwhile standard. I can remember the canings on a Monday morning because I hadn't attended church the previous Sunday, the awful names I was called because of my physical appearance and my family background - names such as 'Guttersnipe' and 'Pig' and 'Scabby'. There is a story to tell about my being called 'Scabby'. One day I was enjoying my favourite pastime of running along the rail of a railway line. I had become quite adept at this and would often challenge other boys to a race; they were allowed to run on the sleepers, while I would run along the rail. This particular day I was running as quickly as I could, missed my footing and fell on to the railway line. I was knocked unconscious, and when I came to I was taken to the casualty department of the local hospital. My forehead was in quite a mess - I carry three scars there to this day. However, I recovered quite well and after a little while returned to school. I had rather a large scab across my forehead and, receiving no medical attention at home, went to school with the scab evident for all to see. During one of the lessons the headmistress, who was taking the class, called me a 'scabby little pig'. I picked up an ink-well and threw it at her with remarkably good aim. She decided that for the well-being of the school I should be punished in front of everybody.

I well remember the large circle of school children and staff in the school playground and the short but extremely fat headmistress taking me into the centre of the circle. She was armed with a cane and intended to use it on me in front of everybody. I had different ideas. It was not that I was particularly tough or rebellious, but I felt humiliated and ashamed. I wouldn't let her get near me. As I walked around the circle, I tried to look for a place near the gate that I could break through. Having found a likely spot, I made a frantic charge straight through it and ran like hell out of that school, never to return.

On to another school. Still tagged as a child from a problem family. Still held to ridicule by other children and often by the teachers. Caught up in a vicious circle of unhappiness at school, truancy, a return to school and unhappiness once more.

It was from one such school that I regularly ran to avoid art classes, for in one art class I had a crushing and painful experience.

I was definitely a non-starter as far as art was concerned, but nevertheless I did what I could. The teacher always seemed to single me out for special attention. She brought my masterpieces to the notice of the class, making ridiculous observations as she did so. One day I had tried to draw an apple. A simple task probably, but to me quite a difficult one. Anyway, I did what I could, and when I had finished I sat with my arms folded. The teacher came along, picked up my drawing, showed it to the class and asked me what it was. When I replied that it was an apple, she said in a very serious voice, 'If I was a maggot I wouldn't touch it.' Like a shot, I replied, 'Well, you should know, miss.' I wish I hadn't said that. She hit me, and she hit me. It was a pity really, because it was in that school that there was the teacher whom I really liked. Still, I suppose it was inevitable that I would have to leave there.

I should tell you something about the teacher I seemed to get on well with. She used to take the English class. I liked writing essays or 'compositions', as we used to call them. I could never understand why she would sometimes give me a penny or threepence after I had produced an essay for her. Perhaps it was because she felt that I was one of the odd ones out in the school. Whatever her reason, it made me feel good, and I used to look forward to her classes eagerly.

One day she asked us to write an essay about a building on fire. I wrote mine as I thought it would appear in a newspaper. When I handed it in she made no comment on it, but a little while afterwards I was asked to report to the headmistress in her office. Experience had taught me that whenever I had to report to the headmistress of any school it was because I was in trouble. I braced myself for whatever was coming. I was extremely pleasantly surprised when the head congratulated me on the way I had written my essay and informed me that she was going to pin it up on the notice board for all to read. This was the highlight of my school life. It may be difficult to understand how I felt, but to me it seemed the only valuable thing I had ever done at school.

I wouldn't want to give the impression that it was only the problems at school that caused me to play truant so often. There were many other reasons. Of course, the instances I have quoted made it that much easier to miss school, but I also felt that it was necessary to do something about our financial plight.

At a very early age I took it upon myself to try to earn some money so that we could get one or two of the things we needed. It may seem hard to believe, but by the time I was eleven years old I was virtually the breadwinner of the family; I wanted to do something to alleviate the sufferings caused by the poverty which surrounded us.

I can't remember how old I was when I first became a beggar. It almost seems as if I had been begging from the time I learned to walk. One of my early recollections was of going around the waste bins left outside shops and looking through them for scraps of food. Stale cakes and bread, pieces of bacon, old fruit, anything that could be scraped out or cleaned. It didn't matter that we would have to cut the mildew off the bread and cakes before we could eat them; it was of far more importance that we had something to eat. I remember too being sent to one particular shop to ask for bones for the dog (we didn't have a dog), and then we either scrounged or stole a few vegetables so that my mother could make a stew.

However, it was begging that I became quite adept at. I considered that it was really earning money. It was obvious that somebody had to do something about providing for the family. My mother was bearing children every two years. All in all, she gave birth to ten healthy children; one was still-born; and she had two miscarriages. We were still moving from house to house with monotonous regularity. We were poorly clad, lived in a state of extreme filth and, with each passing day, seemed to be more of a problem family.

So I took to 'earning' money almost on a full-time basis. As far as I could see, there were three methods I could employ: to beg, to earn money as honestly as possible and to sell goods that I had 'acquired'. I used all three methods. I didn't become a tycoon or anything like that, but I was able to provide a little money so that my mother could buy food and bits of clothing for us. Of course, some of the money went into my father's pocket, but it didn't stay there long before it was handed over the bar of the public house in exchange for a few pints of escape.

One early November, as Guy Fawkes Day approached, I actually dressed up as a guy and sat for hours on end on a pavement while one of my mates collected the pennies. I had a few regular jobs too. Most evenings of the week I was outside the Empire Theatre before and after each of the two performances, trying to change money. The idea was to pester as many patrons as possible to exchange a penny for two halfpennies so that I could put a penny in the chocolate machine. If I only had pennies, then I would ask for two halfpennies for a penny so that I could share with my mate. It was surprising how many people would give me the change required without taking any money from me. Then during the day-time I would purchase flowers from a flower shop at a cheap rate and sell them to passers-by at a little more than I paid for them. There were often old wooden boxes that could be chopped up, made into bundles of firewood and sold from door to door. Also, I would carry cases for people arriving at the local railway station and hold doors open for people going into restaurants and hotels. Then there was the car-minding blackmail. The method used here was to wait for somebody to drive up in a car and run over to hold the car door open for the driver. Then I would ask if he or she would like me to mind the car so that other kids wouldn't scratch it. It seemed that one look at me would convince the person that it would be wiser to allow me to look after it. This usually resulted in a good tip.

It was not too difficult for me to obtain a few coppers through most of these ventures because of the pathetic figure I cut: I was able to stand looking hungrily into a cake shop window until some dear old lady would come up and give me a penny to go and buy myself a cake. I always had to take a while to decide which cake I should buy so that she would move on, and I then would pocket the penny.

Christmas time was a good time of the year. I once stood outside a shop in Newport and watched a little boy have a temper tantrum. He had a parcel in his hand, and he didn't seem to want it. I stood there looking at him and at a lady who I thought was his mother. I knew I looked pathetic and appealing. Eventually, the lady took the parcel off him and gave it to me. I went somewhere quiet and opened it. It was something called a jig-saw puzzle. All that was in the box was lots of small pieces of cardboard; I couldn't see the point of it at all, so I threw it away.

It was at Christmas that I took a lot of personal satisfaction in one form of earning money - singing carols. I loved it. I always liked to sing, and at Christmas time I really enjoyed myself. Mind you, I gave good value for money and always made sure that I had sung a complete carol and was part-way through the second before I knocked at the door. It took a lot longer to get round, but I felt that this was worth doing well. Often I was asked into houses to sing; apart from the financial reward, I was also given a piece of cake and a drink.

I also used to sing for money during the summer months. At the Kingsway in Newport holiday coaches used to stop so that the passengers could have refreshments. I got in with a chap a couple of years older than myself who had a piano accordion. He would play the accordion and I would sing. After a couple of songs outside a coach we would pass a cap around and then go on to the next coach. I much enjoyed doing this, but one day we had a memorable experience. The coach was at the Kingsway when we arrived. It was full of men, and Arthur and myself took up our positions and proceeded to play and sing. We finished a couple of songs, and then I went in to pass the hat around. A man took the cap from me and told me to sit down. We both sat, and the man who took the hat said that as we had entertained them, it was now their turn to entertain us. He announced the name of a Welsh male voice choir, and they started to sing. I cannot speak for Arthur, but I sat there absolutely enthralled. I remember that during the singing of one song two of the men did bird whistles. It was fantastic. When they had finished the man with the cap had the gall to pass it around the coach and then handed it to us. Talk about highway robbery!

I look back on such incidents with a certain amount of pleasure, but there were other episodes that I write about with regret and some shame. It was comparatively easy for me to steal, although there were occasions when I was caught. I had a fairly good contact who could sell the goods I stole, and he would even specify certain items that he required, such as watches, powder compacts, cheap jewellery and so on. I could usually provide these and did so without guilt. Of course, I didn't make a great deal of money on them, but it helped. I can only ever remember stealing one thing that made me feel really guilty. As a matter of fact, this one item caused me a great deal of torment. It was a packet of cream crackers that I took from a lady's basket. I felt for a long time afterwards that the lady may have needed them more than I did. Nobody else in my house worried about my stealing unless I was caught, which brought disgrace upon the family. One amusing incident (it wasn't funny at the time) concerned a turkey. It was Christmas time, and in the market at Newport there seemed to be thousands of turkeys hanging up at the butchers' stalls. I thought that it would be a good idea to try to pinch one of these and began to plan accordingly. I got hold of a butcher's 'S' hook and a large ball of string, went up to the balcony in the market and chose a spot above a butcher's stall. I tied the hook to the string and began 'angling' for a turkey. Before I had got very far, though, I was spotted by the butcher, who let out a loud yell. All hell seemed to break loose, and I had to run from there as fast as my little legs could carry me.

My father was a tough guy. I saw him involved in a couple of scraps and he was very frightening to watch. He stood under 5 feet 4 inches but was as hard as nails. The time to avoid him most was when he went white and gritted his teeth. When this happened it was a sure thing that somebody was going to feel the fury of his fists. Often it was my mother who was on the receiving end. She had some terrible beatings from him. Even now I see my mother with her blackened eye or her swollen, bloody mouth. As for us kids, we were all very very much afraid of his temper. Not that he beat us freely, but when he did it was something to remember. We usually did what my father told us to do. One day I was strolling through the town when I should have been at school. I came face to face with my father. He asked me why I wasn't at school and what I was doing; I told him that I was trying to earn some money. He asked me if I would see him at a certain public house in the early evening. I said I would, and we parted. After spending all day scrounging, I made my way to the public house at the appointed time to meet my father. He asked me how much money I had earned, and I showed him all that I had. He took it from me, and all he said was that I should not tell my mother that I had seen him. I left then and went off to the Empire Theatre to earn some more money. I carried on with my usual evening activities and arrived home very late. Both my mother and my father were waiting for me. They asked me where I had been, and I told them that I had been trying to make some money. They asked me how much I had collected. I emptied the contents of my pocket on to the table. Of course, it was very little, and my mother wasn't satisfied. My father decided to give me a hiding, which he did, with a promise of more to come if I continued playing truant. I can remember another hiding after I had been found out for stealing. He hit me with his thick leather belt all the way upstairs to bed. There were seventeen stairs in that house.

One evening I met a boy about my own age in the town. He looked quite well-to-do and told me that he came from up the valleys. He said I looked hungry and asked me if I would like a bar of chocolate. I said I would, and he gave me a penny bar. He then asked me if I would like something to eat and bought me a meal of fish and chips. He seemed to have a lot of money, but the thing that amazed me was that he had dozens of bars of chocolate. Anyway, it was time for me to go home, and I said goodbye to him. He didn't want me to go because he said he wanted me to be his friend. Before I left him he gave me the large bag of chocolate bars and a handful of money. I felt delighted about this, to say the least. I eventually got home to my father and mother, and before anything could be said I put the chocolates and money on the table. They were surprised and pleased and asked me where I had got them from. When I told them they didn't believe me. They quizzed me very closely. I wouldn't budge. They got very angry and called me all kinds of names. I was a liar. I was a thief. I was everything bad. The strange thing is that if I had said I had stolen the money and the chocolate, they would merely have warned me that I was heading for trouble. It was quite a time before I met that boy again. He was in the approved school when I arrived there.

I still thought of him as a rich boy because I learned that he came from a good home. It wasn't until I was a teenager that I discovered that ordinary working-class people could have houses with decent furnishings. The only time I can remember going into other people's houses was on an occasional visit to relatives, or at Christmas time, when I was asked into a house to sing carols. If the house I entered had good furniture, decent chairs to sit on, nice chinaware or even ordinary cups and saucers, I used to think that the people must be rich to own those things. I remember once asking my older brother what 'slums' were, as I had read the word somewhere. His answer to me was quite simple: 'We are.' He explained that some people were very poor and lived in terrible conditions. Those people were called slums, and that was what we were.

One of the most frightening experiences I had during this time was an occasion when I went scrumping (taking fruit from other people's trees). I went to a big estate on the edge of Newport and squeezed through the railings to get into the grounds. I made my way through the trees, and suddenly my right foot plunged into a hole. My leg sank into the hole right up to the thigh. As it did so, I felt a sharp, stabbing pain in my ankle. I tried to get free, but each time I tried the pain in my ankle was terrible. I started to cry, and then I heard somebody coming through the trees. It was a man carrying a double-barrelled shotgun. I asked him to help me, but his only answer was to ask me what I was doing on the estate. There was no point in lying, so I told him that I was scrumping. He looked at me, pointed the gun at me and said that he couldn't make up his mind whether to shoot me on the spot or just leave me there. After a moment of deliberation, he turned and left me. I was petrified, but I had to get away from there. I made an extra effort and freed myself. Without waiting to examine my wounded ankle, I fled from there as fast as I could. My foot was covered in dirt and blood, but still I managed to move fairly quickly. I carry the scar on my ankle to this day, and I also have in my mind a picture of a man standing amidst the trees laughing quietly to himself as I got free and ran from that place.

All this time I was breaking the law by playing truant from school and getting into all kinds of trouble. I made several court appearances and was put on probation or fined. In the case of the fines I had to pay them myself; I did this by staying away from school and earning the money. It was an endless cycle.

I was frightened as I stood before the magistrates. So that was it. I was going to an approved school. From the court I was taken to a police station in Cardiff, which at that time was being used as a remand home. I have passed there many times since, and I always stop to look up at the barred window and to cast my mind back to the scared face of the eleven-year-old child who had left his family, never to see them all again in the same place at the same time. It was going to be a long time before I would return home; and during the time that I was away, other members of the family would also be taken away from that home.

I don't know how long I stayed at the remand home. It seemed a long time but was probably only a few weeks. I should have learned a lesson from the outset. The policemen seemed to be very big and strong. They always appeared to be watching us, which wasn't difficult because for most of the day we were confined to one room. There were only two rooms for our use anyway. One room was a bedroom, which, of course, we used for sleeping; once we had left there in the morning, we were unable to return until the evening. In the other room we used to have our meals and to sit for most of the day. If I remember correctly, there was a table and some benches. They were all bolted to the floor. Outside was a small yard, where we used to exercise. I think we spent about one hour a day outside; the rest of the time we were restricted to the one room. My parents visited once while I was there. I was taken to a room downstairs to see them, and a policeman was present for the whole of the visit. If we wanted to go to the toilet, we had to knock at the door to the policemen's quarters, and one of the policemen would come in and take us downstairs. Sometimes they were quite annoyed at being disturbed.

One night I saw the eye. It must have been the first or second night I was there. Something disturbed me, and when I looked up from my bed towards the door I saw just one eye. I wanted to call out because I was afraid, but then I could see that the eye was actually looking through a spyhole in the door. At first it seemed to be enormous, but gradually it took on its proper proportions, and I got used to it making its nightly appearance. Not that it only appeared during the night. We sat in our room all day without a member of the staff. From time to time somebody would come in to see what we were doing, but often as we were sitting there, we would suddenly look up towards the door and see that the eye was watching us. It was difficult for us to get into any mischief without being caught. One evening we had got hold of a couple of cigarettes and were having a quiet smoke in the bedroom. The door flew open, and a policeman charged in and caught us. He gave us one hell of a walloping.

There was one boy there who used to go out now and again to run errands for the police. He would also help to do the housework in the police flat. He was quite privileged in lots of ways, and when I asked why he was treated differently from the rest of us I was told that it was because he could be trusted. He left there before I did, but I was to meet up with him a little later on at the approved school and in fact became quite friendly with him. This was a good thing, in my view, because the approved school was to me such a vast place, such a different way of living, that it was useful to have somebody show me the ropes.

I was thoroughly miserable in the remand home. Although I was able to wash and bathe, I was not given any treatment for my terrible rash. I kept the same clothes I was wearing on admission, and these, together with my physical condition, meant that I had to put up with a fair bit of baiting. On many nights I didn't go to sleep before I had had a little cry. Of course, I had to snuggle down into the bedclothes to do so. After all, this was a place for tough guys.

Although I disliked the place so much, I suppose I gained some consolation from the knowledge that I would only be there for a short while, even if the next place was to be an approved school. I thought, surely it had to be better than this, sitting day after day in one room, vacating it only for one of five reasons - exercise, toilet, visit, bed or discharge. Having so much time on our hands with so little to do meant that we spent many hours talking. We talked about the great feats of bravery and daring we had accomplished. We talked about our past experiences with the law. Above all, we talked about our future placements. Some of the boys seemed to know a great deal about approved schools and put their views forward about the best (and the worst) places to go. I must admit that I could not work up enthusiasm about any one of them. I was too scared for that.

I regretted very much the situation in which I found myself and would have done anything I could to alter it. But it was too late. Up to that point I thought that I had lived through the worst. I thought that the days of my humiliations and the cruel tauntings I had received because of my family background, the terrible gibes and the ridicule of schoolteachers were all things of the past that would never occur again. How wrong I was. I may have been lonely and sad, poor and distraught in the past, but I was to endure far worse than this in the future. There were going to be times when I would think that everything I had ever had was taken away from me. There was going to be a Christmas time when I would watch the kids going home for the holiday while I was left behind. (That was the year when one of the popular songs was a song called 'He's the Little Boy that Santa Claus Forgot'. Some other kids stayed there too, and shared with me the compensatory parcels they received from home. I was pleased they did, of course, because I got nothing.) I cried myself to sleep in the remand home, but there were many more tears to follow, many more times that I would be alone and miserable. Quite a number of years were to pass before somebody was to accept me as a real person crying out for help to live a life that was just a little bit worthwhile.

I have tried to tell you in my own way the story as I know it. I wish that I could paint a clearer picture; I wish that I could etch, in words, the misery, the loneliness and the hopelessness that was mine. Not mine alone, though. There were others. There are still those today who find themselves almost as I did, with little or no hope. They wait in fear and foreboding, knowing often that they will be away from their families for many years. How bearable can we make their hell?

It was time for me to leave the remand home because a vacancy had arisen at an approved school. I believe that I was told the day before I was to leave. It rather surprised me when the escort arrived to discover that I would be travelling by train. I thought that I would be going by car or possibly in a 'Black Maria'. As we left, my escort told me that he would like to stop at a shop so that he could buy me some comics and sweets for the journey. We called into a shop near the remand home, and he bought a bar of white chocolate. I remember being intrigued by the fact that it was white. We then caught a bus to Cardiff station, and on the way we chatted in quite a friendly manner. I don't know what we talked about, but everything seemed to be all right. We arrived at the station and waited for the train. Eventually we were on our way again.

It seemed a very long journey. The city was left behind and we were now out in the countryside. Then we had reached our destination. We were at a very small station, and we crossed the bridge with a view of the mountains around us. We walked through the little swing gate, past a pub and two or three houses, one of which served as a little shop, until we arrived at a gateless entrance, then up a fairly long driveway until we came to a gate. It had been a pleasant journey. My escort had been a friendly man. Then came the shock. As we got through the gate, he turned to me and said, 'I'd like to see you run away from here, you sod.' This was the first time I had ever set eyes on this man. What had I done to him to make him talk to me like that? I had caused him no trouble. I had had no thoughts of running away from him and had certainly made no attempt to do so. I hadn't even thought of running away from the school. Perhaps the little bar of white chocolate was his handcuff, and he now felt safe enough to be his true self.

Well, here I was. My escort had departed, and I was left in the place where I was to spend the next three years. I didn't know then what was in store for me. I entered there as a part of a large family; I would leave there to find that the family had been broken up and scattered over a wide area. A lot was going to happen in the next three years; nothing would ever be the same again. One of my brothers I was going to see just one more time.

I suppose it can be said that I settled in 'reasonably well'. For me, as for all the other members of my family who would also be moving from home in the near future, the first thing to be done was to clear up my rash. This was dealt with, but in the process I was subjected to a lot of teasing. At first, I got into quite a lot of fights, but these gradually eased off. This was a strange new world to me, particularly the fact that the school was on the premises. There was a very strict routine, and it didn't take very long to follow what was happening. I liked the school work. Most of the kids there, like me, had lost a lot of schooling, and I became a bit of a shining light in the classroom. I was quite fair at some of the subjects we studied and was in many ways treated in the same way as everyone else. This was a change for me, and I must say that I rather liked it. There were occasions, though, when I was singled out and sometimes, I felt, humiliated. I will mention some of these in another chapter.

Have you ever seen a child in a home or institution longingly waiting for a visitor? We were allowed visitors at the school about once a month. We lived for these days (it was only an afternoon, really). Sometimes I had visitors, but there were times, many of them, when my parents promised that they would come to see me but when the day arrived they just didn't turn up. There were others like me. We looked at every visitor as he or she arrived, hoping that it would be our turn. Sometimes we were taunted by the other kids if nobody came for us. For me this was the case particularly when my parents were in prison. We were often asked on visiting days whether we expected visitors or not. When my parents were in prison I was asked on one occasion if I was expecting anyone to call, then I was told, almost in the same breath, 'Of course, you don't expect anyone.' They were lonely times. What about the days when my parents were able to visit but didn't come? In my mind, while I was waiting, I made up all sorts of excuses for them. I just wouldn't believe that they weren't coming until the very last minute of visiting time. Then, when all the visitors had gone home, I sat and wondered. It didn't matter what anybody said to me afterwards, be it staff or boy; I took no notice. I only wanted to be left alone with my thoughts and tears. I still needed to look out in hope. Eventually, a letter of explanation arrived. 'X was ill.' 'Our money hadn't come through, and we couldn't afford to come.' Whatever the reason given, I accepted it; but if only once, just once, I had been told beforehand that I would have no visit, it would have been so much more bearable. This would have saved me sitting by the door looking out, hour after hour, or pacing restlessly up and down in the yard, or wandering down to the gate to look down the drive, just hoping. Of course, there were times when I had visitors. I was allowed out on these occasions but often got no further than the village pub a few yards outside the school gates; then, after closing time, back to the school, where my father would show the other kids various card tricks and feats of strength. Then it was time for them to go, and I was left alone again for a month or maybe longer. Within three months of my going to the school, my three younger brothers were removed from home. Their ages were two, five, and seven. (This was over forty years ago.) Not long after their removal I was allowed home, and I visited them in a children's home. It wasn't a very long visit, but I suppose I should be grateful because it was a chance to see my seven-year-old brother for the last time. The next time I was to be near him would be six years later. He was lying dead in a coffin, and I was going to the cemetery. The five-year-old I saw in 1945 and then occasionally during the past fifteen years. Recently I have been visiting him fairly regularly. As for the two-year-old, he is now a man of over forty. I didn't see him for the next thirty-three years, when at last I spent a weekend with him. This was a weekend worth waiting for.

About three months after the three boys were removed from home my parents were charged with neglect and were fined £3 or a month's imprisonment in default. They both served the prison sentence, but it was to be for far longer than a month. It's true that they were only in prison for the allotted time, but their punishment lasted for many years to come. I was still in the approved school, and this was the final break-up of the family - a breach that has not been repaired to this day. We were never to be all together again. After the prison sentence my father joined the army. He died in 1946 at the age of fifty-four. He was a broken man when he died, and the words I write are in no way intended to be a condemnation of either him or my mother.

Time went by, and I began to look quite healthy. My relatives told me that I was looking extremely fit. I was quite happy at the school and was used to the routine and the discipline. I kept out of trouble and was made a prefect and eventually school captain. This was the greatest honour I had ever achieved, and I was fearful that I might do something that would mean losing my badge. I had finished fighting. It was no longer necessary for me to get into scraps. My badge carried a certain amount of authority, and the other boys respected this. I hadn't become a saint overnight and still got into some mischief, but never enough to lose my coveted badge.

2 Do You Remember, Sir?

I hope that you won't mind, sir, but I thought that I would write something about you now. Well, you made such a lasting impression upon me that I feel duty-bound to record some of the incidents that occurred while I was at your school.

It may well be that you won't recognize yourself. On the other hand, of course, I may say something that will ring a bell with you. You took on many guises during the time that I knew you. Perhaps you turned up one day as the headmaster. Then on another occasion you were the senior teacher. Then you became the junior teacher, woodwork instructor and even sometimes the clerk. In most of your guises though, sir, you were quite a card. My, how you made us laugh at times.

Do you remember, sir, when I arrived at your school? (If you can't remember my name, it may help if I told you that I was number 5.) Anyway, if you *can* remember, I was covered from head to foot with a rash. I had to be painted every day with some kind of ointment. I didn't know what the rash was, but you had the notion that it was scabies. All I knew was that it was terribly uncomfortable being covered in that awful smelly ointment, with my clothes sticking to my body all day long. Still you cheered us up, didn't you? Do you remember how you used to stand in front of the class and scratch yourself vigorously, remarking that somebody must be spreading scabies around and that you couldn't wait to get home and have a good bath? You were ever so funny, honestly, sir. We all had a great laugh. Well, nearly all of us. I waited until I went to bed to have my laugh because it was then that I laughed so much that the tears rolled down my cheeks. My memory must be fading: I can only recall the tears and not the laughter. The strange thing was that you didn't even know me at that time, so how on earth did you guess that I had a sense of humour? You must have known somehow because there were quite a number of times when your fun-loving cheerfulness came to the rescue.

Do you remember, sir, the time you came into the classroom and I was sitting at the end of the row? You stopped beside me and looked at me, and when I had returned the look you continued on your way. However, you now walked as if you were trying to pull your feet out of quicksand, and with each step you made a great sucking sound with your mouth. All the boys in the classroom hooted with laughter, but as for me, I was just bewildered. Somewhere along the line I seemed to have missed the point. I could see nothing funny in what you were doing. Then I did or said something - I can't remember what it was - but the response I got from you was 'Oh! you are an old stick in the mud.' This, apparently, was another signal for howls of laughter from the other kids. I was completely lost, but you continued along these lines for a few more days, much to the delight of the other boys. I still couldn't understand what the joke was.

Then I was told. My parents had been sent to prison, the children removed from home, and it was reported that the house was so dirty that a person's feet would stick to the floor. While I was being told all this, I could still see you walking past me. I was annoyed, sir. You could have shared the joke with me. Over the years I have thought about this many, many times. It still baffles me, sir. I cannot for the life of me understand why you did this. There were other ways open to you. You could, if you had wished, have been just cruel by telling me in a cold, matter-of-fact way what had happened. I would have cried, sir. Of course I would have cried. I was only eleven years old. On the other hand you could have made a supreme effort and told me in a kindly way, which would have helped me to come to terms with the situation more quickly and less painfully. I would probably still have cried, sir. After all, I was only eleven. You could have kept quiet about it. It wasn't you who told me the truth anyway. So why did you take the line you took? Many incidents in my life have been forgotten. Perhaps I could remember them if I tried hard enough. But this one, sir, I can never forget. You missed an opportunity that day to be kind. You had a chance to help a poor, miserable kid to get over his grief. But you missed out, sir. No, you did more than that. You seized the opportunity to humiliate and hurt. You did an excellent job, sir. You hurt me that day more than I have ever been hurt before or since. You broke my heart, sir, and for this I pity you. I've seen you standing there often over the years; and particularly over the past ten years or so I've thought, as I have looked at you, how rich you could have become, but all I can see is bankruptcy.

You seem to have more understanding as a woodwork instructor, though. Do you remember, at this time, how I sneaked into a corner so that I could be alone in my anguish? Somehow or other you found me. You didn't really know what to say to me. You ruffled my hair and said something about me soon getting over it. I can't remember your words, sir, but I remember your voice and I remember your hand on my head. I thank you for that, sir. Not for what you did, and not for what you said, but rather for trying to understand my sorrow.

Do you remember the smashing holiday we had, sir? Two whole weeks it was, and we enjoyed every minute of it. Plenty of swimming in the pool, games in the park, smashing walks, glorious food and small bedrooms. I liked the bedrooms; they were so much better than the big dormitories.

It was a good school photograph that was taken, wasn't it? I would like to have been in it. As far as I can remember, I hadn't had my photograph taken before. I wanted to look smart for it and spent quite a time sprucing myself up. But you couldn't really be expected to keep everyone waiting for me, could you? I was at least given a privileged position on the sidelines to watch it being taken. I would like to have been in it, though. Still, we can't have things all our own way, can we?

There is just one more incident I would like to recall, sir. It may seem trivial looking back on it, and to me and many others it was trivial at the time but blown up out of all proportion. It was the incident of the six Oxo cubes. It so happened that these six cubes had been stolen from the little shop outside the gates of the school. Perhaps the closeness of the shop to the school added to the enormity of the crime; perhaps the episode reflected a genuine desire to bring the criminal to book. I just don't know. However, after an inquiry that seemed to last an age, I admitted to the theft and was caned; then the incident was closed. I suppose I wish that I could have been caned without falsely admitting to the theft. It was just that we wanted the whole thing to be finished with. It was so tiresome sitting there waiting for someone to own up.

It seems, sir, as if my whole time at your school was filled with bitterness. This is far from the truth, of course. Apart from the fact that I was separated from home, I have many good things to look back on. Considering that it was wartime, we were well looked after materially. We had plenty of indoor and outdoor activities. We learned to play games and spent many a good evening taking part in these activities or listening to the radio. I remember the school concert. I remember singing 'Smiling Through' as a solo. I remember participating in the sketches. I learned to play football there and to swim.

I liked the school work we did. I was quite good at it, and was given plenty of encouragement. One of the thrills of my life was when I entered a competition to write an essay entitled 'The Lodestone'. It was a competition that was entered by many schools in Wales and Monmouthshire, and I won first prize. I was quite proud that day and I felt that the school was very pleased with my achievement. When I became a prefect and then school captain I wore my badge with pride. Oh yes, there were times when I, for one, was very happy.

Perhaps it is because I was far away from home and the events taking place there that I appear to be bitter about some of the happenings at school. I think it's more deep-seated than that though, sir. I've thought a lot about those days, and when I recall the incident relating to my parents' imprisonment I still feel sad and sickened.

I haven't forgotten it - but at the same time I am thankful. Yes, I mean that. There is no need for you to feel remorse. Intentionally or otherwise, you taught me well, and for this I am grateful. Over the years I have had to confront boys whose parents have been sent to prison. I have had to deal with, and clean up, boys covered in rashes, fleabites and even boils. I am not trying to say, sir, that I have known how to deal with them, but rather that I have certainly had experience which told me how not to deal with them. In a way, I am grateful to you all. I know what it is to cry and need help. If I can't help, I can sometimes recognize the symptoms.

Well, sir, I have reminded you of the bitterness, loneliness and misery that I experienced at your school. I feel, therefore that I should offer something in your defence. You were operating in difficult times. It was wartime, as I have mentioned, and our nights were disturbed by the enemy, who had the effrontery to penetrate Wales. (This reminds me that I was a member of your own private cadet force. Remember how we used to carry messages during exercises with the Home Guard?) You were probably short-staffed and were working under a handicap. Your biggest handicap, however, was the fact that you were not nearly as enlightened as we are now, some thirty years later. Training schemes are in operation now, so that many workers in residential establishments of all types are professionally qualified people. The profession itself has grown up. Better facilities and, in many cases, more modern buildings are available. There is a clearer appreciation of the children's problems. Instead of being treated like miniature Al Capones, the children are handled wisely and sympathetically. Whereas in your day approved schools and the like were classed as punitive establishments, this is not the case today. There is a purpose behind children entering such places. No longer are they just held, fed and clothed. They are helped too. Plans are made for their reintegration into society. It is not Utopia as yet, but certainly the aim is a better understanding of the children. The old systems have been done away with. We now try to build what are termed 'relationships' with the children. The days of the humiliation of kids because of the colour of their skins, the sort of homes they come from, their inadequate parents, their own delinquencies, those days are over, sir.

No longer do we have long-drawn-out inquests over the theft of a packet of Oxo cubes. Neither do we employ the system you had of collective punishments. You know the type of thing: something is stolen, so that means no supper or whatever for anybody until the culprit owns up. (Actually, I liked that word 'culprit'. It sounded so high-class.) When collective punishment was the custom the innocent used to feel rather bitter about being punished for someone else. I think we used to accept punishment if we had done wrong; but we abhorred the collective punishments and also the punishments we received when, as far as we could see, we had done nothing wrong. This did happen, you know. Sometimes we were punished for offences that were assumed to have been committed by a particular person, and one of the most galling aspects was the fact that we were often unable to put forward any defence. Still, those days are gone, sir.

Somehow, I don't think you believe me. You may think that somewhere or other these things are still happening. I cannot prove otherwise, of course; my own feeling is that if they persist, then in those places and in that respect they haven't learned much over the last thirty years. It is a pity if this is the case because no matter how much things have been altered by legislation and changing attitudes, one thing remains abundantly clear: that the children we have to deal with are beset with many problems and emotional disturbances. Often these are very painful to bear. It is enough that the kids are left alone to face these things; to me it is tragic if any child is the more burdened by a thoughtless word or action on the part of some adult whose function it is to help that child through his difficulties.

I must say these last few words to you, sir. During the past few years I have learned that caring for children is truly terrific and a satisfying job. Of course, we get kicked in the teeth, figuratively speaking, from time to time, but to me the sheer joy lies in feeling needed by kids who are bewildered, being trusted by them and being looked on as a human being rather than as an awesome figure of authority. You gave me many pleasurable moments, sir. Of this I am sure. It's quite likely that for many kids you did a good job. My only regret is that I remember the incidents I have mentioned. It is not just the remembering I deplore, but more the fact that they happened, to be remembered.

3 They Cared, for God's Sake!

One day I was told that I was wanted by the headmaster and was instructed to report to him. I wondered just what it was I had done and went nervously along to his office. He told me to sit down and then asked what I would do if I was to be given another chance. I can remember the answer I gave him; it was, 'I will take it sir.' I meant every word, I swear that my intention at that moment was that I should never get into trouble again. A date was fixed for my release, and I left his office feeling on top of the world. The day came, and for the last time I went through the gate, down the driveway to the gateless entrance and looked back. I was leaving some good friends behind; this took away a little of the glitter of freedom. But I had with me my railway ticket and a few shillings' savings. I boarded the train and after three long years arrived back in Newport.

It was rather strange that I should get on a bus and sit upstairs in the front because as I approached the district of 'Pill', who should I see walking up the road but my mother. I jumped off the bus and raced after her. It was just as well that I did because I discovered that the family (which by this time consisted of mother, father and sister) had once again moved to a different address. Had I not seen her, I would not have known where to go.

She took me to the new house, and, of course, I was made very welcome. But I hadn't been home long before we were on the move again. Things hadn't changed much after all. I got a job on a farm but only stayed there for one week. Then I got a job in a factory. It was a dirty job that made my clothes smell, and no matter where I went, people around me knew where I worked. There seemed to be no way to remove the smell.

After a little while my sister left home; in a very short while she was followed by my mother. My father and I were living alone. My father was often ill; there was not much money coming in from him. My wages from the factory were very low indeed, and it was quite a struggle for us to manage. My father still managed to earn his beer money helping out in a pub. I had no friends in that area and spent almost all my time on my own, although one evening a week I would go to the cinema with my father. (My father knew the manager of one of the cinemas, and we used to get in for nothing on a Thursday evening.)

The terrible thing, though, was that I had no companions of my own. After paying over my wages to my father and having a little pocket money returned, I was soon broke. I used to hang about the town for hours on end each evening, with no money and no friends. I walked around a lot in those days. I was miserable and lonely. Then my mother came back home, which meant that even my Thursday evening out had to be abandoned. I remember that one of the lads at work once asked me to go with him to a dance. I saved my little bit of pocket money and duly went along. It was a complete waste of time and money. I spent the whole evening sitting on my own. Needless to say, that was the last dance I went to.

Some evenings I stayed at home on my own and listened to the wireless. My father and mother used to go out every evening together. One evening I was depressed. Eventually I went out, stole some money and went to the cinema. I wasn't even careful about it. It was obvious right from the start that I was the culprit. I didn't bother to deny it when questioned by the police. I didn't care any more. The fact that I had to appear in court didn't worry me. I showed not the slightest remorse or regret for what I did. I wasn't afraid, just bewildered and sick. One of the first people I saw at court was my old headmaster. All he said to me was: 'Well, you've done it this time. Now you are really for the high jump.' What could anybody do to me now? The future looked no blacker than what had gone before. Perhaps this would at least be the end of my solitary confinement.

I stood before the magistrates and heard people say that really I was a good boy. The magistrates heard from the probation officer that if they placed me on probation, he would be able to take me to a probation hostel. He had already secured the vacancy. I was told that I would be placed on probation for three years with a condition of residence. It didn't mean an awful lot to me at the time, although I had it all explained to me.

I felt that this was where I had come in - leaving home to begin a punitive sentence. I was now approaching my sixteenth birthday, and what did I have? I had a mother and father who no longer had any of their children with them. I had brothers and sisters who didn't even know me. If you consider the number of houses we had lived in, I couldn't even say that I had a home. I didn't have a friend in the world. I wasn't leaving a girl friend behind. I had never had a girl friend. There was a girl whom I liked a lot at that time; but although I went into the shop where she worked and used to watch her through the window, I was never able to bring myself to speak to her. (On the other hand, I did have kindly uncles and aunts whom I visited occasionally, and they always made me feel welcome.)

I had experienced my share of sadness and loneliness. I cannot claim that I had been fair to others, though, and certainly had not shown much respect for other people's property. It didn't really matter to me that I was leaving home again; I wasn't leaving much behind anyway. I could see what was going to happen. I would be away for six months (although I didn't believe that that was all it would be); then I would come back home, and the loneliness, the sadness, the bitterness, the poverty and the overwhelming feelings of frustration and hopelessness would return; then I would make another journey. Where was hope then? What future was there for me? There is nothing much to lose, I thought, so take me, probation officer, take me away from it all, if only for a little while.

However, if I had known then what I know now, I would have felt less bleak. This was to be the real beginning of my life. What had gone before was going to stand me in good stead in what was to follow. I didn't guess that I was leaving Newport for good; apart from a very brief period, I would never live there again. I would never look at it again through the same eyes.

I was taken to the hostel by the probation officer. We travelled by bus and train, and the man talked to me on the way. This was a different man from the one who had accompanied me to the school all those years before. By that I mean that he was a different kind of man. He didn't butter me up, then leave me feeling deflated. I remember the walk up the driveway to the hostel and I recall seeing the kids working on the land. The hostel seemed close to the village but a long way from anywhere else. It didn't really matter because I wasn't going to be there for long. I was now a teenager, and I was mixing with kids of my own age again.

The hostel was entirely different from the school. There were religious pictures about the place, and morning prayers were held each day, but with none of the 'set pieces' I was used to. (Actually, I was one of the few Catholics who, over the years, were admitted to the hostel, which was run by the Salvation Army.) There was quite a strict regime. We had to get up early in the morning, and there was plenty of work to do on the farm which was attached to the hostel. The food wasn't too good, but it was still wartime, so we didn't grumble about it much. There seemed to be some activity going on all the time, mainly of a religious nature, but it made the days pass quickly. And the evenings were good. There was no television then, of course, but we managed to have a lot of fun all the same.

It was a great period in my life. It was the people who made the place. I met some of the finest characters I have ever met; there was something about the hostel that was infectious. Although we were all lads who had got into all sorts of scrapes and had been picked up and bundled into a little corner of Wales, we didn't feel like criminals any longer. The kids of the village, who were our own age, used to make us feel that, given our circumstances, they would be in the same position as we were. Even today I count many of them among my friends. There was a feeling of warmth towards us. As I write, I think about those days and still feel that sense of comfort that I experienced so often while I was there, a true sense of being wanted.

I will refer to the man in charge of the hostel as the Major, although when I first met him his rank in the Salvation Army was that of adjutant. He was promoted later. As far as this man is concerned, I consider rank to be unimportant. It was he himself who had such an impact on the lives of myself and others, not his status in the Salvation Army. He was assisted in the running of the hostel by his wife, who was the matron, another officer, two male members ·of staff and domestic help.

It is worth noting here that the Major's wife was away when I arrived. She had gone out to the hop fields to minister to the hop pickers - looking after their welfare, making tea, providing first aid, caring for and entertaining the children. She didn't have to do this chore; she chose to do it, and it was typical of her life. I should have been warned then, because years later, when I was in the RAF and spent time off at the hostel, it was not unusual to be called out of bed in the early hours of the morning to go with her to a house in the village where someone was ill or dying. She would offer words of comfort and give any help that she could. There were many such incidents; eventually some of this willingness to help others rubbed off on me. I once spent many hours reading to and tending a retired hairdresser who had been paralysed by a stroke. I cannot pretend that the service I gave was of a high standard, but it was the desire to help others that really mattered. I hope that the atmosphere of the place and the attitudes and warmth of the people will permeate through the words that I write, so that the influence which they had on my life and my future will become clear.

The people at the hostel demonstrated what caring for others is all about - and not just the older folk, the Salvation Army officers and the 'respectable' people from the village, but youngsters like myself as well, the converted thieves, the thugs, the lads who became known as 'trophies of Grace'. It was at that hostel that I went through one of the most traumatic experiences of my life, and there were people there who helped me through it all - adults and kids to whom nothing was too much trouble to help a fellow human being. They were all truly magnificent, and wherever they may be, I thank them. Some of them came back and took the trouble to talk to the boys there. One lad, who died while serving in the forces, wrote an extremely long letter exhorting me to reshape my life under the guidance of Christ. Another died at sea, thereby unwittingly granting the wish of his father, who had said, 'I never want to see the little bastard alive again.' This was the lad who once said to me, 'I *know* I'm a different bloke.'

I will try to describe some of the people who helped me most. First of all, there was the Major's wife. I will call her Auntie. She was a right old dragon at times, but it is rather strange that even now I use that term with affection. When Auntie was on the warpath everybody, and I mean everybody, gave her right of way. But what a woman she was! A frail-looking little woman, thin of face, grey hair tied with a bun at the back of the head, almost all covered by her Salvation Army bonnet. A great preacher who could hold any congregation spellbound. Bouncing with energy, her service for people appeared to be limitless. It didn't matter what time of the day or night she was called upon, she was always willing, always available, to do the best she could. There were a lot of young people whom she tried to help. Apart from the boys in the home, a large number of young people from the village used to go to the 'Army' - to the religious meetings, band practice, youth club and what have you. They all became her responsibility. 'I am your spiritual mother,' she used to say. She would talk to the kids for hours on end. If any one of them had a problem, she would take time out to talk to him individually and to guide him through his difficulties. It sounds trite, but that was literally true; she always found time.

You see, this was what life meant there. This was how we were viewed. We were boys in a probation hostel. All of us had been in some kind of trouble to have been placed there, and yet there was no differentiation made between us and the boys and girls of the village. Our backgrounds probably differed from theirs. Our outlook on life was different. Some of us had a nasty taste in the mouth from past experiences. Many of the young folk of the village had jobs and worked for wages; we worked within the confines of the hostel for pocket money. They would come and go almost as they wished; we were allowed out only one afternoon a week. They were being looked after by their parents; we were not. But to Auntie we had two very important things in common. First, the children in the village and the boys in the hostel were young; and second, they were all people. How many times we would hear her say, 'Oh, my dear young people.' 'So what?' you say. I'll tell you so what. We suddenly felt just a little bit important. To someone we mattered. We counted for something. Look at little Reg in the small Salvation hall. Auntie, who was conducting the meeting, asked that somebody should read out a verse of the hymn. Watch little Reg as he slowly rises to his feet to read the verse. Come and sit next to me and I'll quickly and quietly tell you that he cannot read a word. We don't laugh; we cross our fingers for him. He holds the hymn book in front of him and reads these words:

> I have not much to give thee, Lord,
> For that great love which made thee mine,
> I have not much to give thee, Lord,
> But all that I have is thine.

We want to applaud but probably consider it irreverent. Little Reg sits down, and just before we sing the words Auntie says, 'Very nicely read, Reg.' Yes, we know Auntie has told a fib that day, but Reg has obviously spent some time memorizing the words. Surely no one would want to take away that beaming smile from Reg's face by disclosing that she had told a lie?

Then there was Ginger. Ginger had left the hostel and was working on a farm some miles away. One day the Major received a phone call to say that Ginger had been taken to hospital, critically ill. He had no parents, so Auntie felt she had an extra responsibility. She believed greatly in the power of intercessory prayer, and apart from getting together her own prayer group, she also called on some young people from the village to form small groups to pray for him. I remember one Thursday evening when she had been told that his condition was very serious. She immediately held a prayer meeting in the crowded kitchen of the hostel. It doesn't matter what I may think about religion and prayer now; there could be no doubting the sincerity of the people who were praying, though some of them were probably praying for somebody for the first time ever.

Although Ginger got over the crisis, he was still quite ill. One day Auntie said that she would like to have a chat with me. More often than not, when she said this the butterflies in our stomachs worked overtime, and we questioned ourselves about what we could possibly have done wrong. However, on this occasion she told me that she thought that Ginger was grateful to her and the Major for their visits to him in hospital. He was always pleased to see them, but at the same time she felt that he expected them to visit, possibly out of a sense of duty. She told me that she knew I wanted him to recover, which indicated that I cared about him. Why not show him I cared by visiting him myself? The hospital was about ten miles away from the village, and the only day that I could visit was a Sunday. I checked on the bus timetables and discovered that I could get to the hospital all right, but it would be extremely difficult to get back. The only answer was to walk. Ginger was so pleased to see me. Auntie was that kind of woman.

And there was Gran. Tough, hard Gran. Gran was a huge woman who walked with a peculiar gait, as if she had to drag one side of her body. She often seemed to be grinning from one side of her face only. She smiled fairly often, but more often she was very serious. She was responsible for the catering arrangements at the hostel and was a bit of a hoarder of food, almost as if she was always expecting to fall on hard times. Because of her size and peculiar walk, if she was displeased with someone she would appear to approach them at breakneck speed, like a great mountain. She did this to me on many occasions when I was working in the kitchen. Of course, had I hung around long enough, I might have found out that she was nothing like as fearsome as she seemed. Nevertheless, whenever there was an argument and she charged towards me I was a big enough coward to get out of the way as smartly as I possibly could. After a little while, when I thought things had cooled a little, I would return, and she would say in a matter-of-fact way, 'I suppose we had better get on with some work.' Just that. No recriminations, no nagging, just acceptance of the situation for what it was worth. There were times, when we were peeling potatoes, or scrubbing the floor, or washing up, when we could talk to Gran. She didn't say an awful lot in return but seemed to be interested in what we had to say. When one of the boys was going through a rough period she wouldn't treat him gently or offer advice; she seemed to back-pedal with the boys working in the kitchen and didn't push them as hard as she normally would. I once saw her weeping about one of the boys. She lived in a large bedroom on the premises, and rumour had it that she was quite well off financially, but she would not hesitate to send the boys along to her bedroom to fetch something for her. This made them feel that in spite of their murky pasts, they had come to a place where they were trusted. It was all part and parcel of the place. She was really a grand old soul, who contributed a lot to the establishment and to the boys. It was a sad day when she left the hostel, and sadder when she died.

I really don't know what pseudonyms to give the next two people. They were marvellous characters, like music hall stars. They were two sisters-in-law who lived in the village; both were married and had families of their own. Each attended the hostel's religious services and played a very important part in weekend visits to other Salvation Army corps. Whenever we went to evening meetings in places within easy reach, they came along. We used to take part in religious plays, and it was their responsibility to see that we were dressed ready for the parts we were playing. I couldn't put that in any other way, because to say they were 'dressers' in a theatrical sense would be nothing short of ridiculous. However, they did a marvellous job; they chivvied us and chased us, even to the point of giving us hefty shoves from time to time. There was never any malice in their treatment of us, never any singling out of one particular child for their displeasure. More often than not, they appeared to be flustered, but they were always cheerful and spent many hours chuckling in retrospect. These two ladies were as different as chalk and cheese. One was very timid and quiet, the other almost masculine and very strong-willed. When the stronger one got moving everybody moved. The quiet one was pushed around by her too, but they seemed to work marvellously well together. Their brand of humour was fantastic; their words of encouragement and their help were given unstintingly. I want to thank them both. They meant a great deal to myself and others like me. We had many a good laugh with them, and up to that time some of us hadn't had a lot to laugh about.

There was another character living in the village. He was quite a handyman and was consequently roped in to do odd jobs in and around the hostel, such as building walls and so on. When he was working there, although he had his own job, he often had a boy to help him. I was fortunate enough to help him on many occasions. His language was shocking. The first time I heard him release a stream of obscenities and profanities I was absolutely staggered, not so much because of his language, but more because of the surroundings. Here he was, in the grounds of a Salvation Army hostel, swearing like the proverbial trooper. He used to say that if they wanted his help, they would have to accept it from him as he was. He used to drink fairly regularly and smoked quite heavily. The boys at the home were not allowed to smoke, and I can never remember him giving a cigarette to any of the boys who worked with him. Neither can I recall any of the boys asking him for one. The time eventually arrived when I was to go into the RAF. Apparently, this chap was most put out when he discovered that I would be going to the railway station on my own. I now know that he said to someone, 'If he was my son, I would take him to the station to see him on the train. This kid is away from his family. Somebody should go with him.' He came with me. A small incident perhaps, but indicative of the feelings of the people with whom I came into contact in those days.

These people and many more like them, both at the hostel and afterwards, gave me a welcome and an acceptance I had never had before. Although none of them was a qualified social worker, they really cared.

4 I Almost Called Her 'Mum'

The hostel accommodated twenty-four boys, who were all on probation. They came from every part of Britain. I hadn't been there a day before I was being shown the ropes and having explained to me what the place was all about. This was done initially by the boys, of course. They always seem to manage to get in first.

One of the most interesting things I was told by one of the boys was that if I wanted to get on in the place and become a blue-eyed boy, then the easiest way was to be 'saved'. Now, I had never been a churchgoer, apart from the occasions when I was compelled to attend, and my religion up to that time was Roman Catholic. I just didn't have a clue what he was talking about. He explained that the hostel, being a Salvation Army place, held religious services throughout the week, and often an invitation was extended to the boys to kneel at the Mercy Seat, which was at the front of the congregation. This was the place where you asked Christ to forgive you your sins and you then become 'saved'. According to my informant, this act pleased the Major and his wife a great deal; being 'saved' carried with it a number of privileges, and therefore you couldn't go wrong. I can't say that I was very enthusiastic about the idea because I wasn't very keen on church services anyway. Well, the first time the Major chatted to me you can imagine my feelings when he said that it was possible that some of the boys might have told me that the easiest way to get on there was to be 'saved'. He went on to say that he agreed with what I had been told, not because it carried any privileges, but rather because being 'saved' meant being changed and living a better and more useful life through Christ. Because of this, one got on better wherever one went. It was still all foreign to me, but I could see that the man was sincere and believed in it himself. Yet he certainly didn't push the subject down my throat. As for me, I still wasn't particularly interested.

However, we had our share of religious services. Each morning we had family prayers. One of the highlights of these prayer sessions was the reading of the remembrance book. This was a book that was signed by each boy on the day that he left the home. Sometimes this was done on the Sunday before a boy left. The usual procedure was that during the Sunday evening service the Major would announce that the boy would be leaving during the coming week. The boy would choose his favourite hymn and then, during the singing of it, would walk to the front of the hall and sign the book. Whichever method was used, the important thing was that the boy's name went into the book. Each day at morning prayers a page of names was read out, and we were asked to remember the boys and to pray for them. It was still war time, and many of them were serving in the forces. At first, although it was rather an impressive part of morning prayers, the ritual didn't really mean an awful lot to me, but as time went on and some of my pals left the hostel, it began to take on some meaning when their names were read out of the book. I soon found myself thinking of the boys I knew, and although I probably wouldn't have admitted it at the time, I may even have said a silent prayer or two. The Major would also announce items of news about the boys who had left the hostel; I will never forget the feeling we had when told that one of them had been killed in action.

There was usually a service of some sort each evening. Some I went to, but others I didn't bother to attend; they were optional anyway, and one or two special evenings didn't interest me at all at that time. The Major took great delight in 'selling his wares'; this he would do by telling us stories of old boys who had made good, kids who had been as bad as, if not worse than, we were. I soon met some of them, and they certainly seemed to be doing all right for themselves. I was impressed by it all. I was so thoroughly fed up with the way things had been up to that time, that I longed desperately for something better. I felt good in this place. I felt as if I was trusted. This was a new and strange experience for me, and I was rather pleased about it. People from the village used to come into the services. It was great to feel that we could mix with them, and that they didn't look upon us as freaks but were prepared to take us as they found us. I made many friends among them and look upon them as my friends to this day. Only recently I went back to the village and was treated almost as a long-lost brother.

During the daytime we worked on the farm or in the house doing domestic work. We scrubbed and we dusted and we polished, and then we waited to have our work inspected. The Major's wife usually did the inspection, and if the work you had done passed the first time, you could consider that you had indeed done a first-class job. Mind you, she had an uncanny knack of going straight to the very place where you had forgotten to dust. Another job to be done was collecting pig swill once a week. This meant getting out the horse and cart and going to the neighbouring town to collect up the vegetables and fruit that folk were going to throw away. If this was your job, then it meant that you actually went out three times a week - once collecting swill and the other two occasions selling produce from the farm. I liked doing these jobs because I met so many people. They all seemed to know the man who was in charge of the produce, and, of course, it was rather novel for me to serve customers, to take their money, to hand them their change and so on. I used to enjoy these jobs even when the weather was atrocious, as it can be sometimes in South Wales. There was something about the work that gave me a warm feeling. Occasionally, we were taken to the cattle market in a town some fifteen miles away. I enjoyed this too, and here again everybody seemed to know the Major. We would go in the van and would often be accompanied by pigs that were going to be sold. It was fascinating to find out about the goings on at a market. Sometimes the Major's wife would decide to go along as well. On these occasions she would go shopping, and the boy or boys who went were usually asked to go with her. It was on one of these visits that I saw some beautiful china for the first time. She loved pretty things and spent long periods in a china shop in the town. I used to get rather bored with this but still admired all the beautiful articles in the shop.

The days went by, and I was happy. The food was fair; we had pocket money to spend each Saturday; and I had a smashing suit that I was able to buy in a shop. That was a great day for me, when I went to get the suit. I didn't have much choice, but there were three things I liked about it: it was new; I had bought it in a shop; and it was mine. It was the same kind of feeling you get when you buy your first car.

It was noticeable how many of the boys gave their 'testimonies', explaining to us how different they had become since being 'saved'. Old boys returned to tell us how fine it was to be a Christian and to live a fuller, richer life. 'You must be born again,' the Major repeated time after time. I often wondered if this was the answer for me. I don't think it would have mattered what I was offered at that time; I just wanted to be different. If it was religion that I needed to be different, then so be it. So one morning I went to the Mercy Seat. I didn't feel any different afterwards, but I was helped and guided. I was told to read my Bible and other pieces of helpful literature that were given to me and to pray. I was encouraged to speak in meetings. I became quite good at it - at least, so I was told - and I began to believe in Christ and His teachings.

The time was approaching when I would be leaving the hostel. It came much sooner than I had anticipated. Although the condition of residence was for a period of six months, I left the hostel after just four and a half months. There were some at the time who remarked that I had reached the status of blue-eyed boy. What actually happened was that the Major had suggested that I should go to Reading, where he could fix me up with a job and lodgings. I decided that this was what I would like to do. It really wasn't a very difficult decision to make because I figured it this way. First, I had no friends in my home town, and there was a distinct possibility that I would be able to make friends in Reading - for a start, there were two former boys from the hostel already working and living there. Second, there was the fact that my father was displeased because I had, by this time, joined the Salvation Army. Furthermore, this could possibly be the break from my old ties that I had been waiting for, and, of course, I would remain in contact with the people at the hostel. All in all, it added up to a chance to make something out of the wreckage of my young life.

So the day came for me to go to Reading. Arrangements had been made for me to work with a builders' firm owned by a family of Salvationists. The lodgings that had been found for me were also with a family of Salvationists. When I arrived at Reading station I was met by the local Salvation Army officer, who made me feel welcome and then took me to my lodgings. When we got there the officer breezed into the house, while I walked in rather sheepishly, with my back pressed against the wall. I cannot say why, except to point out that in those days I found great difficulty in speaking to people when I first met them. (My friends would probably not agree, but even now I sometimes have the same problem.) I stood there, feeling rather awkward, while I was introduced to the people in the house. There was a middle-aged, married couple, their two daughters and a young girl of about eleven who used to live there for quite long periods. They appeared to be a very homely family, and the two girls seemed pleased to see me. Of the two daughters, one was a girl about seven years older than me who had been confined to a wheelchair for most of her life. The other was about a year older than me. (Although I determined that the people I wrote about should be anonymous, I also made up my mind that I would mention the girls by name because of all the people I have met in my life these two were most definitely among the tops. The girl in the chair was called Nellie, and her younger sister was Kathleen, known to all as Kathy.)

I was overwhelmed at first. Here was I, in a normal household with a normal family, being asked simple questions such as 'What do you like to eat?' and 'Do you like a cooked breakfast?' I had never experienced this before and was a bit nonplussed by it all. But they were able to make me feel at ease, and I was treated almost as one of the family. Several incidents occurred while I was living with the family that I think bear repeating.

I hadn't been there long before I was taught a wonderful lesson. Nellie was extremely friendly to me right from the start, and one day, after I had returned from work and had eaten my tea, she asked me if I was any good at arithmetic. I replied that I wasn't very good but could manage the basics. She told me that she couldn't add up at all and would dearly like to learn. I ended up by volunteering to help her. It wasn't much, just simple addition and so forth, but little as I had to offer, here was someone worse off than myself who would gratefully accept that little. To her it was wonderful that I should give up my spare time to help her. To me it was one of the first occasions when I felt that I was being helpful to somebody else.

Then there was another heart-warming incident. My bedroom was in the attic, and each night as I went up to bed I passed the room in which Nellie and Kathy slept. One night as I was on my way up to bed I heard Kathy calling my name. She wanted me to go into their bedroom. I didn't know what to do. I was happy living in that house, and I didn't want to run the risk of being told to leave. I looked into the room and saw that both girls were in bed. I asked Kathy what she wanted, and she begged me to sit down on the edge of her bed. She held out her hand, invited me to take it and asked me to talk to them. Then she said: 'You see, Tom, Nellie and I have always wanted a brother, and we would like you to be ours.' A little while later their parents peeped into the room and saw me sitting there. They just said, 'Goodnight', with a gentle reminder to me that I had to be up early in the morning and shouldn't be too late in getting to bed.

And finally a triumph. I was still attending the Salvation Army services at that time. Each Sunday one of the young people attached to the Salvation Army Corps would ask the others to tea before the meeting. These teas were usually fabulous affairs in spite of wartime austerity. Everything was done in a proper manner, and I always felt extremely privileged to be included. Kathy had taken her turn to invite the fifteen or so young people to their house, and one day her mother said to Nellie, 'It's your turn to invite next week.' Nellie was tickled pink and took great pleasure in inviting her guests in spite of her difficulties. Her beaming face was a joy to see. Then one evening, when I was helping Nellie with her arithmetic, the girls' mother turned to me and said, 'Do you know, Tom, I really think it's about time for you to invite people to *your* house for tea.' I was over the moon. I invited everyone to our house, and I felt wonderful. I haven't called anybody 'Mum' since I was eleven years old, but if there is one person to whom I'd like to give that name, it is that woman. I remain deeply grateful to Nellie and Kathy and their parents, and I bitterly regret any subsequent disappointment I caused them.

Life in that family was great. I was very happy. I had a good job; I lived in a wonderful household; I had more friends (including a girl friend) than I had ever had in my life. So I ran away. I went to the railway station and boarded a train to Newport.

It is rather strange that this should have been the first and the only occasion that I ran away. I don't know why I did it. All I can say is that although I wanted a change from my home circumstances and realized I would probably be better off away from home, there were times I felt that there was an enormous pull towards home. This may well have been the case when I ran away from Reading, I don't know. It is curious, to say the least, that although I had decided to go to Newport, when the train eventually arrived there I stayed put and travelled on to Cardiff. When I got there I had nowhere to go. Consequently, I spent a couple of nights sleeping rough.

I felt cold, miserable and very lonely. When I left Reading I had some money with me and, apart from running away, had not been in any trouble. I phoned the hostel and spoke to the Major, telling him where I was, and in a very short time was on my way back to the hostel. The Major had a long chat with me and eventually said that I could stay at the hostel for a short while. This I did and some time afterwards went into lodgings in the village. Again, I was lucky in so far as I was made welcome by some wonderful people, and this was to be my home until I was called up for the forces. A lot was to happen before that time though, and it was going to be brought home to me most forcefully how caring all these people were.

By this time I had become completely engrossed in my activities with the Salvation Army. I was speaking frequently at meetings and was getting a lot of bookings to speak at other centres. I visited different towns with the Major and his wife and spoke at meetings all over the country. Often a party of young people would spend weekends conducting evangelical meetings in places as far away as Yorkshire.

I remember that one Easter weekend thirty of us had been booked to conduct weekend meetings in Batley. These young people comprised the 'Singing Company' or children's choir attached to the corps of the Salvation Army hostel. I was a young man at this time, and although I didn't sing with the 'Singing Company', I would help out with the meetings by singing solos, reciting monologues and sometimes giving the address or sermon.

We went from South Wales to Batley by coach, and it was a long, long journey. Many of the younger children were rather ill on the way, and I did quite a lot of cleaning up.

We had a great weekend. Although a lot of hard work went into the weekend meetings, we considered it all worth while. So to the return journey. I didn't really relish the idea of having to do a lot of cleaning up on the coach coming back, so we decided to tell the children to sit on newspaper. This, we told them, would reduce, almost eliminate, the possibility of feeling sick. I also took it upon myself to tell jokes and to lead sing-songs. Believe it or not, we did this for the whole of the return journey. We arrived in Wales feeling extremely tired, but the coach was in a very clean state. People who made that journey so many years ago still talk to me about it when we meet.

I had some very proud moments in the Salvation Army. Because of the deprivation of my early years, I got a great thrill from being noticed and considered important. I suppose one of my fondest memories is of a meeting at the Regent's Hall in Oxford Street, London, conducted by the late Albert Orsbome. At that time he was the General-Elect of the Salvation Army. I was to give a recitation at the meeting entitled 'Holy Ambition', and the last verse started with the words: 'And I might be the General one day, who can tell?' This was always a good time for a laugh, and the folk at this meeting were no different from any others. It was when I finished that the General came over to me, placed his hand on my shoulder and said, 'And you might be the General one day, who can tell?'

On another occasion I was asked to be one of the guest speakers at a mass rally in Trafalgar Square. This was attended by many high-ranking Salvation Army officers and thousands of Salvationists. It was a tremendous thrill for me to approach the microphone and address that great throng. Later on a large picture appeared in the Salvation Army paper, the War Cry. I have the photograph still.

I was meeting a lot of people and visiting more places than I had thought possible. At the same time I was beginning to think of others, of people in need. I was helping to minister to the sick and to help those in trouble. Behind the change in me lay the influence of the Major's wife. And my thoughts turned to my own family. I had to know where they were.

I made some inquiries and eventually found out where my three younger brothers were living. They were in foster-homes in Shropshire. Freddy was in a foster-home on his own, and Terry and Dennis were on a farm nearby. I started to write to them. I wish it had been as easily done as I have just described. But how do you sit and write to brothers you haven't seen for six years, especially as they were only two, five and seven when you last saw them? Do you write: 'Hiya, kids, I'm your big brother, sorry I haven't seen you around lately?' No! You sit and think. You write and then screw up the sheet of paper. Your hands get clammy, and you start again. So it goes on. You write a short letter at first, post it and then wait. You hope that they will reply. It's like making a blind date; you just don't know what to expect. The replies come, and you feel a little easier. You write back and get more replies.

One day I received a letter that made me feel a little uneasy. The letter appeared to come from Freddy, who was in a foster-home with a Mr and Mrs Pickering. It stated that Dennis and Terry were not very happy at Bank Farm. They were not getting enough to eat. Dennis did not look very well and had missed going to school on several occasions. The letter also said that Freddy had some misgivings about the situation and suggested that somebody from the Welfare should check to see that everything was all right. (Some years later, when I spoke to Freddy about this letter, he said that he couldn't remember writing it. Unfortunately in those days I did not keep letters in a safe place, so I cannot prove that I received it.)

I wrote back to try to get more information. I was told that the children had been visited and were all right. This was in December 1944. On 9 January 1945 I walked through the village to the hostel. I was feeling pleased because it was my birthday. Dennis was lying dead in Shropshire.

He had died as a result of the terrible treatment which he had received at the hands of his foster-father. I couldn't take it in. I refused to believe it. I didn't even know him. I felt the loss more acutely because I didn't know him than I would have if I had shared my life with him. The kid had never even lived. He had been shifted around for years after being removed from home because of the neglect of his parents; now, at the age of thirteen, he lay dead, beaten and half-starved by his foster-parents.

I was lucky. I was surrounded by friends who saw me through the days that were to follow. They helped me - both people older than I was and youngsters of my own age. If ever I regretted anything that I had done in the past, it was then that the regrets were most bitter. I kept telling myself that if things had been different, I might have been with my brothers when they were taken away from home. I might have stayed with them and, being older, might have been able to help them. An awful lot of 'mights'. It is quite possible that events would have turned out exactly as they did anyway.

I learned that the farmer was to be charged with manslaughter. Several people asked me if I was going to the trial. I told them that I would have liked to meet my brother Terry and to see what sort of a man this farmer was, but that I wouldn't be going. I gave them no real reason for my decision.

The fact was that I couldn't afford to go. It wasn't just a case of not having the cash; other things, like loss of work and having to pay for my lodgings, prevented me. Now, in the hostel there lived an old woman (at least to us she was old). She was a bit of a battleaxe. I never got on very well with her and spent a lot of time arguing, much to the displeasure of her husband. She was a right old moaner. Even her humour was sometimes barbed. She took me aside and asked me if I was going to Shrewsbury, where the trial was to be held. I told her that I wasn't but didn't give a reason. She then told me that she wanted me to go, and that she would pay my fare. I had to explain that it was more than just a question of the train fare, and so she saw to it that my lodgings were paid for during the time that I was away from work. (We argued just the same afterwards; she still moaned at me, and her humour was just as barbed.) You can see now why I consider myself to be so fortunate in meeting such great people. She is dead now, so I can make known this secret. I went to Shrewsbury, but the trial was transferred to Stafford, and I only managed to catch a glimpse of Terry but saw nothing of the farmer and his wife. I didn't go to the trial at Stafford. When it was all over I tried once more to find out where Terry was, but because of the publicity the trial had received, his whereabouts were kept secret.

I was still taking part in Salvation Army activities. One weekend we were scheduled to conduct meetings at a corps in Cardiff. One facet of the Salvation Army is their open-air services. This particular weekend we had just completed an open-air meeting and were marching back to the Salvation Army hall when I saw two young boys who had come out to listen to the band. I looked at one of the boys and he stared straight back at me, so I went across to him and said, 'Excuse me, but are you Terry O'Neill?' He said he was, and then I said, 'Well, I am your brother, Tom.' He merely said, quite quietly, 'Yes, I know.' And that was it. That was exactly how it happened. I often look back on that day now and just wonder. How did he know it was me? I had seen plenty of pictures of him in the newspapers, but as far as I can recollect, he didn't even have a photograph of me. He cannot say either. When I asked him again a short while ago his answer was, 'I don't know how I knew. I just knew.' Of course, we were so delighted to see each other, and he took me straight to his foster home to meet his foster-parents. They were fine people and had a family of their own. They made me feel welcome, and I was allowed to visit him on subsequent occasions and to take him out. On a couple of occasions I brought him back to the hostel, and he seemed to enjoy the visits. Then for some obscure reason he was moved once more, and it was a long time before I saw him again.

Time passed very quickly. I was old enough now to be called up for National Service. Because of my past I had some difficulty in getting myself accepted for the RAF, which was my choice, but managed it eventually. (A strange coincidence is that later one of the boys who was in our home experienced the same difficulty when he applied to join the RAF. It is hard to live down the past.) I completed my National Service, then went on to the Salvation Army college in London to train to become a Salvation Army officer.

It was a wonderful experience for me, and I can remember well the feeling of warmth when I was asked to do something that was apparently unheard of up to that time. A party of cadets (students) were going to Colchester to conduct an Easter campaign. I was among that party, and the captain who was leading the party asked me if I would be prepared to give the address at the main meeting of the weekend. All this may seem of small significance, but to me it all added up to one thing - acceptance.

I believed sincerely in what I was doing, and I cherish my memories of those good days. But I had been a Salvation Army officer for only a short time when I left the Army. There were several reasons for my decision; I won't go into them in detail except to describe one incident, which marked the turning-point.

I was commissioned as a probationary lieutenant and was sent to a Salvation Army corps in North Wales. After I had been there a few months I took some leave and went back to the hostel. I spent an extremely busy but enjoyable holiday there. On my return to North Wales I had to change trains at Shrewsbury. Instead of waiting for my connection I left the station and went to visit the farm where Dennis had died. I remember climbing a hill and looking over to where I thought the farm might be.

It would be useless for me to try to explain how I felt that day. Mere words could not express my grief, my hatred for the farmer and his wife, my contempt for the authorities under whose noses Dennis's death had occurred. I was sick - sick of everything that had happened to me and my family, sick of the very life I had lived. The experience was traumatic; I was not equipped to deal with it at that time.

I wandered about for a day or two, aimlessly, and eventually found myself back in Newport. Back home with my mother; my father had died, and my mother had remarried. Of course, the Major sought me out and pleaded with me to return to my work with the Salvation Army, but my mind was made up. I would never be able to overcome my early setbacks; it seemed inevitable that I should have to face up to my past over and over again. I didn't stay at home long. Within a week or two I had joined the RAF again. My days as an active Salvationist were virtually ended.

At the hostel there was a girl whom I rather fancied. She wasn't on probation; she worked there. We had been going out together for some time, and just after I went back into the Air Force we were married. She was well aware of the quality of the bargain she was getting, but she married me just the same. I've tried to explain that after entering the hostel I met real people. She was one of these although she was very young at the time. These were people who didn't give a damn what you had been; they were more concerned with what you could become. Anyway, we got married, and I finished off my time in the RAF. I settled down to normal married family life. I worked in the coal mines and lived near to the hostel. I did a lot of spare-time work at the hostel, and there were even occasions when my wife and I would sleep there so that the Major and his wife could have a holiday.

The Major and his wife were continually telling us that we should consider taking up residential child care work. They felt that there was a great deal that we could offer to deprived children. But I was loath to enter the work. My own background and upbringing held me back. Still, the folk who knew me were convinced that this was the kind of work for which I was suited. I remained reluctant. They persisted but couldn't push me. They did, however, cause me to give the idea a lot of deep thought. Then a vacancy occurred in a children's home. The home was going to close in six months, and the vacancy was only for that period. I talked it over with my wife, and we came to the conclusion that my background should not stand in the way because, strangely enough, it was the only qualification I had. We applied and were appointed; that was in 1956. After that we worked in three children's homes, and even now I like to feel that the experiences I suffered as a child have stood me in good stead in dealing with the problems of the children with whom we have worked.

When the Major died in 1970 I was still doing that work. I attended his funeral, as I had his wife's two years earlier. As I watched his coffin being lowered gently into the grave, with his cap sitting proudly on top of it, I said a silent 'Thank you'. It took him a long time; it caused him a lot of heartache; it meant many long hours of work; but he eventually succeeded. He finally managed to make me believe in myself. There were countless other boys he helped in this way too. He made us realize, through the example of his own life, how unimportant we were. He showed us that there was a lot that we could do to help others; that beside some of these people's problems, our own paled into insignificance.

It is comparatively easy for me to understand some of the problems facing the boys with whom I have worked because I have had to face some of these problems myself. He was different. He was brought up in a posh home. He wanted for nothing as a youngster. His family were well-to-do and were respected in their neighbourhood. There are even roads named after his father. He didn't have to face up to any of the problems that confronted us, yet the strange thing is that he seemed to understand; more important, having understood, he cared.

5 The Stranger I Know

One of the most significant events of my recent life occurred when I was on my training course at Cardiff. Part-way through the course it became common knowledge that I was brought up in care and that my brothers had spent a number of years in foster-homes. Each student had to complete a project during the course. A fellow-student, Bill, decided that he would do a project on foster-homes. One day, while he was discussing his project with his tutor it was suggested that Bill should talk to me about it in order to gather some information at first hand; trying to be helpful, I suggested that I would have a chat with my brother, Terry. Terry had spent a number of years in foster-homes and had experienced many different facets of fostering. He had been moved around, often without being given a reason. He had been treated kindly, and he had been treated abominably; who better to talk to than him?

During the previous ten years or so I had visited Terry maybe once or twice a year. These visits usually lasted anything from fifteen minutes to an hour. We talked about the weather, our respective jobs and other cosy snippets of chit-chat. We said our fond farewells until the next visit. By this time he had a wife and two daughters. On each visit we met as strangers and parted as strangers until the day I went to see him about the project that Bill was working on. I asked him if he could possibly give us some information on foster-homes and his experience with them. He wasn't particularly interested but agreed that if he could help, he would. One interesting point was that he said that there were some things that he would never talk about. We had a short chat, and we made arrangements for me to call again in a few days' time to have a longer discussion. A few days later, at 7 p.m., I called in to see him. We started by exchanging our usual pleasantries, and then we began to talk about each other. The amazing thing was that he didn't even know that I too had been taken away from home. This knowledge seemed to break down the reserve that existed between us. We recounted many stories from our early childhood, and even then there were many gaps left. It staggered me to realize that until that evening he himself did not know the circumstances behind his removal from home. It became a very poignant meeting. We talked until 2 a.m. When I left his house that morning I was leaving behind a brother that I had met for the first time in thirty-three years. I recognized that I had a sister-in-law and that upstairs, sleeping in their beds, were my two nieces. The ball was beginning to roll and nothing was going to stop it.

During our conversation that evening Terry remarked that he had tried to get back into the army but he was told that he was now too old. This was rather significant because he was already aware of this rule. It seemed to me that he had been trying to make a journey into the past. He agreed with me that this probably was the case, so I asked him outright. 'Well, how far back do you want to go, Terry?' His reply was immediate. 'All the way, right back to Bank Farm.' Perhaps I shouldn't have said what I then replied. I told him that I would take him back. We would go back together one day. It was just what he wanted to hear. Over the next week or so we made plans and eventually settled for a Sunday in July.

The days and weeks went by. The appointed Sunday was approaching, and Terry appeared to be calm. As for me, I became so tense that I was a burden to all with whom I came into contact. Terry said much later that he thought at one stage that I would back out at the last minute. I knew that despite everything I would be there. The day eventually arrived, and we started on our way. I was quite calm now; it seemed as if it was Terry's turn to be tense. He would argue this point, but it was noticeable that he had developed an irritating little cough, coupled with a hoarse voice. He said that it was the brand of cigarettes that I was smoking. (On the return journey his voice had returned to normal and his cough had disappeared.)

The day itself was symbolic of our early lives - miserable, cold, wet, with occasional outbreaks of sunshine. We went together along the road that he had travelled some thirty years earlier. He was a man now, no longer a frightened, bewildered little kid, uprooted from his home and family. In 1972 we were returning to 1940. We went every painful step of the way, and at each milestone he rolled back the years. Sometimes, as I watched him, I could see that he was looking through the eyes of a child. He remembered small things that delighted him, incidents that frightened him.

Our family had been a cause of great concern to the National Society for the Prevention of Cruelty to Children for a considerable number of years. In December 1939 the family were found to be living in appalling conditions and our parents were prosecuted for neglecting their children. They were found guilty, and, unable to pay the £3 fine, they both went to prison. The four children were removed from home on a Place of Safety order. All four children were covered in a rash, and the first step was hospitalization. Afterwards they went to a children's home and remained there until May 1940, when they appeared in court and were committed to the care of the local education authority. They were placed in a children's home again until a suitable foster-home could be found. The girl was eventually placed in the care of her maternal grandmother. The education authority advertised for foster-parents. Because the boys came from a Roman Catholic family, an undertaking was given that they would be brought up in their own faith. There were eleven replies to the advertisement, only one being from a Roman Catholic. After references had been taken up it was decided to place the three boys with this applicant, a lady. Then a series of events began which was to culminate in the abject misery of two of these boys and, in the case of one, death.

The three boys were Dennis, Terrence and Frederick. At the time of their removal from home they were aged seven, five and two respectively. Terry cannot remember a great deal of what happened at this period. He does, however, remember being taken to the children's home after being in hospital for a while. He told me of one amusing incident that occurred while he was at the home.

There was rather a high wall around the house, and people passing the home would have to walk alongside this wall. After the boys had been there for a little while they had the idea of hanging a child's bucket over the wall and collecting pennies from passers-by. It was quite a rewarding dodge until, inevitably, they were caught; then it was a matter of course that they should be punished.

It was soon time to move on, to a place near Hereford. Here was their first foster-home. Terry remembered the time when they were travelling there by bus, and he spotted the conductors coloured tickets fixed to a board. Terry was fascinated by the wads of coloured tickets and thought that he would like them for himself. He promptly stole them, causing quite a lot of trouble when the conductor couldn't find them. Nobody seemed to be able to help the conductor. Terry innocently went on his way, and it was not until they reached the foster-home that Dennis, finding the tickets in Terry's pocket, brought the whole incident to a head by informing all and sundry about what Terry had done. Their foster mother was very angry; it wasn't a good start in a new foster-home. This incident had no bearing on the fact that the boys were here for a very short time, however. The reason was that their foster-mother was suddenly taken ill, and the boys had to be removed. This time the local education authority contacted one of the eleven original applicants. The people concerned were willing to take the three boys, and although they were non-Catholics, they agreed to the boys being brought up within the Catholic faith and undertook to see that provision was made to this end.

So the boys found themselves on the move again. This time their destination was a small village not far from Leominster. This was to be a very happy time for them. To these kids, and to Terry in particular, the house was like a palace. They had never known anything quite like it before. To reach it they had to walk up a long, winding lane with green meadows on each side. They came to a large farmhouse, in the front of which was an orchard. The family here consisted of father, mother and three sons. Although so young, the three newcomers were well-trained and knew their proper place.

They addressed the man of the house as 'sir', the lady as 'ma'am' and the three sons by their Christian names with the prefix 'master'. They were happy here because the people were kind to them. They were boys, of course, and often got into scrapes of one sort or another.

Quite close at hand stood a castle. At the time this castle was being used as a Catholic boarding school for girls. There was no other Catholic school in the area, so it was arranged that Dennis and Terry would be allowed to attend the school daily. Although they were only two boys among so many girls, I have yet to hear Terry complain. I recently visited the school on Terry's insistence. It has now been returned to its proper station as an ancient monument, and it is open to the public. We paid our forty pence admission, and from then on I must admit that I have never before experienced such a conducted tour of an ancient monument in my life. We didn't see the paintings, the carpets, the candelabra, or the furnishings. I was shown the classrooms, the headmistress's study, the place formerly occupied by the desk at which Terry sat to do his lessons. We wandered around the grounds. Here stood a tree, the same tree which Freddy, who joined them at the school later, was helped to climb, then found that he was unable to get down. The other two boys left him there until he was eventually helped down by somebody else.

This school boasted a percussion band. To Terry this was something out of this world. He wanted this band for himself, so he did the only thing that he could think of to get it. He pinched it. Piece by precious piece he took it home until he had the whole band safely hidden away. He recalls that he joyfully played the triangle every step of the way home. His joy was short-lived. At home the band was discovered and the nuns at the school were informed. The band was returned, and Terry had to accept his punishment which was, to his amazement, just a token smack. He has told me that he didn't mind the punishment. He didn't resent the fact that the instruments had to be returned, because in his own words, 'for a little while they were all mine.'

As he recounts the incidents and adventures of those days there is a positive gleam in his eyes. They twinkle with mischief. He tells of the day when his younger brother fell into the pond. Terry fished him out, and then they stripped off and tried to dry their clothes in the sun to avoid discovery. He remembers the day he fell off the tractor, and the tractor ran over his legs. Afterwards he had to tell nasty vicious lies to avoid further trouble. He recalls the time that he ran away from the foster-home. He had been up to some mischief and his foster-mother was going to wallop him. He ran out of the house, and she chased after him. She tried to coax him back into the house, but it took a long time for him to relent. Even then it was only after his foster-mother had promised him that he wouldn't be smacked when he returned. Once he was inside the house she broke her promise, but Terry didn't mind too much about that.

We stood just outside the house. The people didn't live there any longer. He pointed out to me where they slept. He told me that while the family had their meals in the dining-room, the three brothers ate in the kitchen with the maid. He recalled that the food was plentiful and excellently cooked. There was no bitterness in his voice. As he talked, I could understand why. Although he recalled the humorous events, the naughty escapades he was involved in, one could see that underneath there had been happiness during that period. He didn't have to explain to me. In the light of subsequent events and, indeed, of events leading up to this time in their young lives, this had been, for the three brothers, more than three years of living in a nice, happy foster-home.

Then his eyes lost their twinkle. There was sadness in them. They had to leave this foster-home. They didn't know why. They had done nothing wrong. Why did no one tell them why they had to go? They were happy there. Could no one have soothed some of the hurt they were experiencing just by telling them why it had to be as it was? They were just told one morning that they wouldn't be going to school because they were on the move. In only a few short hours they would leave their home. One day Terry and his younger brother would return to look at it and remember. But not Dennis. The education authority had made arrangements for the three boys to be fostered with a married couple in Shropshire. However, complications were to arise because the foster-mother concerned had been approached by her own local authority to accept another foster-child, a little girl. She had agreed to this, and the girl was taken in. The foster-mother wrote to the boys' local authority explaining what had happened and pointing out that she was now unable to take the three boys. Furthermore, according to the 1933 Children and Young Persons Act, it was not permissible for the three boys to go to the same foster-home as a girl. The escorting officer was in a quandary because he was asked to try to persuade the woman to change her mind and accept the three boys anyway. The escorting officer took the boys to Shropshire in the hope that he would be able to do this.

The foster-mother was adamant. She would take the youngest child but not all three. She eventually agreed to take the two younger boys, but Terry only for a very short time. This left the escorting officer with Dennis. The lady recommended that he try a nearby farm. The escorting officer duly took Dennis off to the farm but met with no success there either. The farmer suggested that a Mr and Mrs Gough at nearby Bank Farm might well be willing to take the lad. The officer moved on. At Bank Farm he did not inspect the sleeping quarters but satisfied himself about the condition of the living quarters and asked the Goughs if they would take Dennis in. They agreed to do this and filled in the necessary forms that the escorting officer produced. It was a relieved officer who patted Dennis on the head, telling him to be a good boy, and made his departure. A week or so later Terry joined Dennis at Bank Farm.

The youngest brother remained at his foster-home. The three boys were now apart from each other for the first time. Frederick would see the other two from time to time but never again would they live together. The youngster was now about seven years old, and he remained in that foster-home for the next eleven years. He assumed the name of his foster-parents and was later to become a professional man and to create for himself a very successful life.

I did not meet Freddy until he was thirty-five years old. During the summer of 1972 Terry and I went up to the north of England to stay with him for a weekend. We arrived late on a Friday night. We rang the doorbell, and I swear that I heard a hurried movement towards the door. Then there was a short period of quietness; the door opened, and Freddy stood there, smiling. Terry said hello in a way that showed that he was pleased to see him. Then Terry introduced us to each other. We shook hands and smiled at each other. We were introduced to his lady friend and given coffee and sandwiches, and then we sat down to talk. It's surprising what you can find to talk about after thirty-three years' absence. We talked about the journey there. About his work and mine. We talked about sport and our plans for the weekend.

The next morning Freddy cooked us breakfast. We ate it; we sat and smoked cigarettes; we talked. To hell with the weather now, to hell with sport and our work: we talked of us. We talked for a very long time indeed. There was so much to say now. Freddy told me that for years he had thought that his entire family consisted of the three boys. He knew absolutely nothing of his other brothers and sisters or of his parents. We adjourned at lunchtime. We were taken to his lady friend's house, where we were made welcome by her family. Freddy told us that they were getting engaged in the near future, and we toasted them with champagne. (His young lady told us afterwards that her family were suitably impressed by his two brothers. That was nice to know.) We talked again on the Saturday night. His young lady was present on this occasion, and we thought at first that she might be upset by what she heard. This was not to be the case. If anything, their relationship was strengthened by her presence during these disclosures. We talked until the early hours of the morning. We continued on Sunday morning. Then it was time for us to leave. Freddy's parting words to me were: 'You won't wait another thirty-three years before you see me again, will you?'

For Dennis and Terry things worked out differently. Dennis was killed by cruelty and neglect. To this day Terry bears the scars of years of terror, torment, bewilderment, loneliness and sadness. In spite of a succession of ghastly experiences, he remained in care, moved about from one place to another without an inkling of the reasons for his committal to care. Sometimes he will laugh and shrug it off and say that it wasn't all as bad as it is made out to be, but still he lives with his experiences. I know that he suffers deeply every time he hears of a case of cruelty to a child. As he was once provoked into writing in a letter to a national newspaper: 'Was no lesson learned? Must it happen again?'

6 What Happened in November

I don't think that I would have volunteered to take Terry to visit Bank Farm had I not thought it important that he get it out of his system. Here we were in 1972, making our way there with some trepidation, trying to put the clock back some twenty-seven years. I was trying to capture in my mind the torment and suffering two little kids went through all that time ago, wondering whether this visit would have an adverse effect on either of us. Actually, it turned out that I was only furnishing for Terry the picture that he had carried in his mind for all those years. We experienced a little difficulty in finding the village in the first instance, but it was soon obvious that he was back in an area that he knew well: this was where he had lost his clogs; be careful here - there is a ditch; we had to go through a ford in those days to reach the farm. Small details that went through his mind as we made our approach to the farm. It began to rain. The countryside looked bleak. Suddenly we were there. I could not take note of our location; the only thing I noticed was that the farm appeared to stand half-way up a hill. It looked remote and desolate.

There were people in the farmyard - a man, a woman and a boy. We got out of the car, and I told them who we were and the purpose of our visit. We were greeted with a certain amount of suspicion; our questions received non-committal answers. The man told us that he hadn't lived there very long and consequently didn't know much about the past history of the place. We had come a long way, through a long period of time, and we were not inclined to be put off as easily as that. The man, who was doing all the talking, maintained that he knew nothing of the O'Neill boys. Then he pointed towards a lorry that was jacked up in a barn and said, 'Perhaps he can be of more help to you than me.' He called out a name, and another man appeared from under the lorry. He told us that he remembered the boys. When I introduced Terry to him the whole atmosphere of the meeting changed. The attitudes of the people living in the farm altered, and we were able to talk. We asked for their permission to enter the farmhouse, and it was granted.

At first Terry was confused. Changes had been made, and it appeared difficult for him to get his bearings. Then suddenly it all made sense to him, and he volunteered pieces of information about the structure of the farm as it was when he had been there. The redecoration that had been carried out together with the alterations could not hide from him the place it once was. There were the cubby holes. In there was the pig bench. Here was their bedroom. I saw what he showed me, but only that. He saw far more. He was seeing again the marks on his back where Dennis had clawed and pinched him during that fateful night as he cried in agony with the pain caused by the pummelling he had received that evening. He saw again the policeman who came to take him (Terry) away from the farm. He remembered that he cried out as he was being carried, 'Don't let them take me away, Dad.' He is horrified to this day by the possibility that it might have been construed as an earnest desire to be allowed to stay on the farm. In fact, he assures me, he cried out because of the fear that had been instilled into him of the dire consequences of being removed from there. After all, some five years previously had he not hidden behind a sofa to escape from being carried away from home by a man in uniform? He was petrified on that occasion, and he was petrified now. I am jumbling the story again. I must go back to the beginning of this episode.

Dennis had gone to Bank Farm, and a week later it was decided that Terry should join him. Terry cannot explain why, but he didn't want to go there. He pleaded with the people he was with to allow him to stay. He even suggested that it would be better for Freddy, the youngest, to go with Dennis. However, it was not to be, and Terry eventually went to Bank Farm. Everything seemed to be going well at first. The kids romped around the farm, attended school regularly, and appeared to be quite fit. Mrs Gough wrote a letter to the education authority saying what good kids they were and expressed the wish that she be allowed to keep them there.

Then came November, and the scene changed dramatically. Dennis did not go to school quite so regularly that month, and he was seen by a neighbour to be walking with a limp. Admittedly, this was probably due to the fact that he was suffering from chilblains. However, there appeared to be a marked change in the pattern of Bank Farm. Throughout the months from June 1944 until November 1944 things seemed to be fine. Mrs Gough saw the boys' headmaster quite often and discussed them with him. What, then, went wrong? Why, some eight months after his arrival at Bank Farm, should Dennis be slowly winding his way up Stow Hill in Newport, peaceful at last, in his coffin? Why was he so light at thirteen years of age? There was no pain now in that frail body of his, but undoubtedly the marks of violence were still visible.

I have spent many hours poring over newspaper reports of that time and of the events that reputedly took place. I have talked to Terry and have visited the farm. I have seen the room where it was said that Dennis was tied to a pig bench and thrashed, while Terry was made to stand near at hand, holding a lantern so that Mr Gough could see what he was doing. I have seen the place where the kids would stand to receive their accumulated 'strokes' with a stick for their wrongdoings. Terry said that it sometimes amounted to 100 strokes. Mr Gough argued that it never amounted to more than fifty. Does it really matter which one was right? I have seen the place where the cubby holes in which the kids were locked once stood. During the subsequent trial comparisons were made between the size of these cubby holes and that of a telephone kiosk. Apparently, one of the boys would be locked in a cubby hole, while the other was receiving his strokes outside; when the punishment had been meted out their positions were reversed. One thing I haven't seen is the trough in the yard where Dennis was made to wash and scrub himself. Remember: this was at the beginning of a bitterly cold January. The trough had a thin covering of ice. Dennis was forced to wash himself while he was naked. Then he had had to run back into the house to receive his beating. And the cow whose udders Dennis used to suck is no longer there.

I am confused.

I look at a newspaper report for December 1939 that describes the home in which Dennis lived as 'indescribably filthy'. I move to 1945 and read that a person who visited the home where Dennis lived said, 'I have seen some bad homes, but this beats the lot.' A doctor compared it with some of the worst slum homes he had been in. When Dennis was taken away from home in 1939 he was dirty. He was covered with sores and a rash, but he was fairly well-nourished and he was alive. When he was taken away from Bank Farm in 1945 he was dirty. He had septic ulcers on his feet. His legs were severely chapped, a condition for which he had received little or no medical attention. His chest was extensively bruised and discoloured. He had recently been beaten on the back with a stick. His stomach contained no trace of food. He was dead.

Perhaps it would not be too difficult to apportion blame. Reading through the reports of the trial, the inquest, the public inquiry, time and again one comes across an amazing series of misadventures. People who should have dealt with various aspects of the boarding out of the children were sick or on leave. The brothers had to leave one foster-home because of sickness; another suddenly became unavailable because of a confusion between two authorities. The children were visited less frequently than they should have been because of differing rates of remuneration for fostering between one authority and another. The reports of the officers who did visit conflicted, and reports were accepted from visiting officials who were unqualified to assess the conditions in which the children were living. The placement at Bank Farm was made by an escorting officer rather than by an officer responsible for boarding out. Many reasons were given for these administrative failures, some of them justifiable: it was wartime, and the authorities were short-staffed; large number of evacuees from the cities had taken up much of the available accommodation in country areas. It would serve no purpose now to point an accusing finger.

When I listen to Terry as he describes what he and Dennis had to endure or when I read the newspaper accounts of the trial of Mr Gough, I always wonder what went wrong. Things went reasonably well at first. The boys helped on the farm. They appeared to be well cared for. They played games with their foster-parents on occasion. The food they were given was monotonous, to say the least, but it was adequate and regular. At first they slept on comfortable beds; then two other foster-children moved in, and Dennis and Terry were given another room, where they slept on palliasses on the floor. Their bed coverings were reported to be quite inadequate. The other children were there for a short while only, and after their removal Dennis and Terry were once again the only two foster-children on the farm.

They were alone. They were two kids living away from their family, with little or no idea where they came from, who their parents were or whether or not there were any other members of the family. They were well aware, of course, of the fact that they were in a foster-home. At times they were quite naughty. They would take a long time over tasks that they should have carried out far more quickly. They were reputed to have kicked the chickens as they fed them. It was even said that they were seen to kick the calves. The two brothers were known to have fights with each other, and on one occasion were reported to have been armed, Terry with a stick and Dennis with a shovel. So they were certainly not angels. It was suggested that in view of behaviour such as this, it was right and proper that they be punished. Be that as it may, there cannot possibly be any justification for the type or the amount of punishment that was meted out to them. Apparently Mr Gough had a totting-up system. As each boy committed an 'offence', he was told that he would receive a certain number of 'strokes' for it; at the end of the day Mr Gough would call the two boys, tell them how many 'strokes' they had to come and proceed to give them the allocated number with a stick. Towards the end of Dennis's life this became a daily occurrence.

Mr Gough was the person who carried out this form of punishment. Mrs Gough was never in any way responsible for the beatings they received, unless, of course, her complaints led to a certain number of strokes being 'awarded'. She never carried out any beatings herself. She was eventually charged with 'exposing the said child in a manner likely to cause unnecessary injury to health'. However, she certainly did not care for them as she should have done. When Mr Gough was sentenced to serve a term of imprisonment of six years, Mrs Gough was also sent to prison. Her sentence was six months.

The days of the brothers' sojourn at Bank Farm were drawing to a close. The punishments continued, but, according to Terry, more sinister happenings were taking place. Terry will talk for a long time (at least, he did to me) of Mr Gough appearing at the bedroom door late at night dressed as a ghost and making weird, ghostly noises, until both the lads were near to hysteria, or of Mr Gough getting the boys out of their bed in the early hours of the morning and sending them out into the darkness to protect the animals from the ghosts. On one occasion they were even called from bed in the early hours to pick blackberries. Terry told me that on one dark night he woke the boys up and sent them outside to see that everything was all right; when they were called back in Mr Gough was waiting for them by the door. They returned in single file, Dennis in front. As Dennis went into the house, Mr Gough, who had covered a broom with a white sheet, caused it to fall between them as if it was a ghost coming at them. Terry tells of many such incidents.

One picture appears quite vividly in my mind. I see Dennis - poor, thin, bruised, pained, hungry Dennis - standing by the table, looking longingly at the food that was being eaten by the others. There was to be none for him. He had had his fill. Had he not stolen the occasional swede? Had he not had the audacity to steal from the pantry? To think that he had the gall to steal the milk from the cow's udder! Sometimes I just sit and think about this boy, my thirteen-years-old brother whom I never knew. I think about his life at home, his removal, his wanderings, his sufferings, both physical and mental, his death. When I think of his death, I remember his funeral. At the time of his funeral we didn't really know about the cause of his death. We only knew that we were not allowed one final look at the body. I recall the hearse and the car. The car was occupied by his father, his mother, his eldest sister and myself, the hearse by Dennis. As we made our way slowly up Stow Hill in the direction of the cemetery, we were unaware of the fact that in one of the houses on the hill was a young girl fifteen years old. She was in care and in service. She asked to be allowed to go the funeral but was refused permission. So she waited, and she dusted a window ledge until she saw the hearse coming up the hill. In her own way, she waved goodbye. We were a large family, Den. She was your sister.

Dennis is dead. I will let him rest in peace. The events of Bank Farm are now history - history which in this case must never be allowed to repeat itself. Den, perhaps it was expedient that you should have died. Mr Gough's cruelty may have been instrumental in ensuring a better deal for children in care. We still grieve for you; we still deplore the circumstances in which you died. We will never really understand.

Among the things which puzzle me most is a statement made by Mr Gough. His words ring in my ears: 'Of the two boys, Dennis was my favourite.'

7 Preferential Treatment

So far I have dealt with events in Terry's life leading up to and including the period at Bank Farm. Initially, we had intended that he would write the next part of the story himself. The reason for this was that he once lived in a foster-home in Cardiff, and it became very special to him. He was most emphatic that he wanted his foster-home to have a special mention, and that his true feelings towards the people should not be lost in the recounting of this part of his life. Unfortunately, although he made some valiant efforts to commit his memories to paper, on each occasion he seemed to 'freeze'. Nevertheless, during our talks he provided me with many details of his wanderings; I will try to tell his story accurately in my own words.

After his removal from Bank Farm Terry was taken to a children's home. However, the superintendent in charge of the home considered that Terry was in too bad a physical condition to be admitted to the home. Terry was taken to another home and was accepted in this one. Of course, it was obvious to all concerned that Mr Gough was to be tried for the offences he had committed, and that Terry was to be a principal witness at that trial. Terry, therefore, was very much pampered in the home and could do no wrong. He was protected, even over-protected. Looking back on this period, he claims that, as far as he was concerned, he was placed in an unenviable position. The other children in the home, not knowing the circumstances surrounding his admission there, considered that he was very much a pet. Often they would report him for the slightest misdemeanour, apparently hoping that he would be punished. He received no punishment, which must have been very confusing for the other children. Terry had to stay at the home until after the trial, which eventually ended in April that year.

At first, the trial was to be held at Shrewsbury, but after it got under way it was decided that for various reasons (local anger towards the Goughs was one of them) that the trial should be transferred to Stafford Assizes. Terry travelled to the court daily.

Of the trial itself he doesn't remember a great deal. Looking back on it, he was a little confused about how long the actual proceedings took. He seemed to think that it lasted for weeks, when in actual fact it was over in about nine days. The confusion arose in his mind because for him the ordeal lasted from January to April. This included the inquest, the preliminary hearing, the committal to the Assizes and the transfer of the trial from Shrewsbury to Stafford. His own anguish was very real, and he spent a total of almost five hours in the witness box. He broke down on several occasions and was treated most sympathetically by the judge.

There spring to Terry's mind two incidents concerning the trial that he can remember with any clarity. The first was in the courtroom, when the defence counsel for Mr Gough suggested that some of the injuries inflicted upon Dennis were caused by Terry while he and Dennis were fighting each other. Terry is sure that he heard somebody in the crowd murmur, 'Oh! the dirty little murderer.' Terry has never forgotten this and is still hurt by the fact that somebody could even have *thought* that this was the case. He may have misheard, of course; but the incident is a pointer to what Terry has had to live with for so many years.

The second event that he recalls is, in retrospect, rather amusing. It happened while he was walking along a street one day. He was suddenly approached by a mountainous woman who had a very loud voice. She asked him if he was Terry O'Neill. When he answered that he was, she burst into tears and, after a little while, proclaimed to all and sundry, 'If Gough were here now, I'd kill the bastard myself.' At the time it was far from funny, because as a small eleven-year-old he was frightened by this very large woman with a booming voice and very upset.

The trial was over. Mr Gough was sentenced to six years' imprisonment, and Terry returned to the children's home. He received many letters from all over the country, and messages of sympathy were included among them. Letters arrived from a lady in Australia, and for a good number of years afterwards he received Christmas cards from her. Soon the trial receded into the past, and Terry remained at the children's home. It wasn't too long, though, before he was on the move again, to another foster-home in Cardiff. One cannot know what went through his mind at that time, but, with his previous experience, he must certainly have had misgivings about going to another foster-home. He couldn't possibly have realized that this was going to be so different.

From the outset Terry's new foster-family made every effort to give him a real home - not only material benefits but also the one thing that had been missing for many years: love. He was accepted as part of the family. I saw him several times during this period, and he was a normal child. He would charge into the house after playing outside as if he belonged there. From the eyes of his foster-mother there shone a light as she looked at him as if he were indeed one of her own. The boys in the house, her own sons, looked upon him as one of themselves. They didn't spoil him. If he did something to upset them, they told him off for it. Everything seemed to be so natural. This could have been a very trying period for all concerned, but it turned out to be one of the happiest periods in the whole of his lifetime. He still visits them on occasion.

There was one difficulty. Terry's new foster-parents wanted him to call them 'Mum' and 'Dad'. Now, this was far more demanding than it would seem. Terry could never make himself do this. You cannot just 'acquire' a mother and father. Of course, Terry would have loved to have called somebody 'Mum', but it had to be more than a word; it had to be an expression of feeling. There were occasions when his foster-mother would ask Terry to tell 'Dad' that his meal was ready. Terry would go upstairs and make a noise so that 'Dad' would be facing the doorway as Terry went in. This ruse relieved Terry of the burden of prefacing his message with the name 'Dad'. The boy had to cope with the same embarrassment when he had to speak to 'Mum'. This may be difficult to understand, but the emptiness created by loss of contact with real parents is not very easily filled. They were not his parents, and although he had almost no recollection of his real parents, it was virtually impossible for him to regard these fine people wholly as substitute parents.

Up to this time Terry had experienced a very hard and sad life. He had had his share of physical hardship and punishments. Yet, in spite of everything, he can recall only four times in his whole life when he really cried. One of the occasions was in this house. He had been involved in some small mischief, and his foster-parents had reason to chide him. They ticked him off and sent him to bed. He went to bed and cried. He cried because they didn't want him. Admittedly, it was only a temporary banishment, but to him it was a real rejection. He wished that they had thought of any alternative; to cast him away from them on this occasion was painful in the extreme.

Terry was growing up, and he wanted a bicycle. A very old one was acquired that needed a lot of repair work to make it roadworthy and presentable. He took it along to a local cycle shop and asked the man if he would do it up for him. He was told that it would cost a lot of money to put right, but the man promised to do it as cheaply as he possibly could (he knew Terry's foster-parents very well). The amazing point was that the man repaired the bike and charged Terry the princely sum of two shillings and sixpence. Terry was absolutely delighted with his very own bicycle.

It was during this time that Terry kept company with a gang of boys whose pastime it was to go into the city centre and steal from some of the shops there. The first time Terry went out on one of these escapades he had no idea of what was required of him. He stood inside a shop, and one of the other lads suddenly said, '.Tally ho!' This was repeated a few times, and then it was suggested that they all go outside again. It was explained to Terry that this was the means of telling him the coast was clear and that it was safe to steal something. They went back into the shop and once again the word was used. Terry, who had his back to the counter, turned around and took the first object to hand. This happened to be a rather large cuddly toy and he couldn't hide it inside his jersey. They ran through the shop, and all the time Terry was trying to conceal the toy. Eventually, however, he had to drop it to avoid being caught. So much for his first adventure in big-time shop-lifting.

One day a very strange thing happened to him. He had been into the city centre with the usual crowd of boys and had been successful in stealing a toy diver. The crowd of lads returned to their respective homes, and Terry had said goodbye to them one by one. Now he was getting close to the road in which he lived. His fingers curled around the diver in his pocket. When he arrived at the comer of the road, fingers still holding on to the toy, he stopped and stood in one spot for what seemed an age. He remembers clearly his thoughts on that occasion. This is what he was thinking: 'What I have in my pocket is stolen. If I get caught, I will be punished, and if that happens, it won't hurt me as much as it will hurt the people in that house. They don't deserve to be hurt. They are too nice to be hurt. I should be the last one to want to hurt them.' He threw the toy away, and that was the last time that he ever stole anything.

I picked up a newspaper one day and was quite surprised to see a picture of Terry staring at me. The picture was of a contented little boy. Underneath was the caption 'Terry smiles again'. Alongside the picture was a short article stating that Terry had settled happily into his new foster-home and had learned to smile again. It mentioned some of the events that had occurred prior to his moving into the foster-home. Not long afterwards Terry was moved once more. No reason was given, but Terry said that he was given to understand that it was to avoid further publicity.

He had come far, but he had a long way to go yet. He would spend the next few years in children's homes, but he was unaware of this at this time. All Terry knew was that he was very happy in the foster-home in Cardiff and didn't want to go anywhere else. He was in care, though, and whoever ordained that Terry should be moved on probably knew best the reasoning behind such a step. So

Terry went into a children's home. By this time he should have been used to the fact that he would be moved around. However, he stayed in this children's home for nearly two years, and then he moved into a home for senior boys so that he could take up some training for his future working life.

It was while he was in the children's home that an incident occurred that he will always remember. I must stress that this incident occurred *after* his experience at Bank Farm. Perhaps the person in charge of the home was unaware of what Terry had endured at Bank Farm. He certainly seemed to have no knowledge of the fact that Terry had sat at a table eating a meal while his starving brother had to stand by and watch. Had he known this, surely he wouldn't have done what he did to Terry. Even without this knowledge, there is still no excuse for the action taken. Terry was accused of some small misdemeanour (if memory serves us right, the crime was smoking). Terry denied that he had done this terrible thing. The man in charge was convinced that Terry was lying and told him that unless he owned up he would get nothing to eat. Now, Terry was always a stubborn boy. He had become inured to physical punishment. He would soon own up and accept his punishment when he had done wrong; if, however, he knew he had done no wrong, there was absolutely nothing that anybody could do to get a confession from him. It was certainly so in this case, and the person in charge was true to his word. Each meal time Terry was asked to own up, and each time Terry would deny the charge.

I must admit that I find the next part of the story hard to believe, but, knowing something about institutional life in those times, I have grown to accept it. When he first told me about the incident Terry was adamant. He begged me to believe that this ritual went on for three days. At breakfast time on the third day he was asked the question again and gave the same answer. He went in expecting to get something to eat but was shocked when he discovered that he had to stand and watch the other children eating. After breakfast he was asked again, and again just before dinner. Always he replied in the same manner. Once more he stood and watched the children eating their meal. By this time other members of staff were pleading with him to admit that he had been smoking, all to no avail. At tea time the same procedure was followed, with the same result. After tea he was asked once more. Upon giving the same answer, he was told that he could have some tea and that afterwards the person in charge would like to see him. Terry had his tea and then went to see the person in charge. The man told Terry that in spite of all his protestations, he still believed Terry was guilty and that he would have to be caned. Terry's reply was something like this: 'If you really think that I did it and caning me will make you feel better, then you had better cane me. But don't expect me now or ever to own up to this crime because I didn't do it.' Terry was caned.

About this time there was another occasion when Terry cried. To him staff at the children's home were simply staff - some kindly, some authoritarian, but all remote. One day a young man came to the home to be a housefather. He seemed to get on extremely well with all the kids there, but Terry sensed that this young man was different, in so far as he seemed to have time to talk to the children, and they felt that they could talk to him. Terry probably didn't realize, but a very strong relationship developed between them. One day Terry committed some small offence, and it fell to this young man to deal with him. Terry did not deny having done wrong. The young man gave Terry a verbal blasting, and then the incident was closed. The very next time that Terry saw this young man was when he came into the house with some of the other children. He walked straight past Terry without even looking at him. The boy was shocked. He wondered why anyone should shun him for doing one small wrong. He could accept the ticking off he had received, but to be cast aside because of it was more than he could take. So he found a quiet corner and cried.

Later that day he came face to face with the young man, and Terry asked him outright why he had ignored him. Terry was not ready for the answer he received. It was simply: 'I didn't see you, Terry, honestly.' Not a very exciting incident to recall perhaps, but an illustration of what people working with children can mean to those in their care. Terry has not seen this man since leaving the children's home, but he still speaks of him with a great deal of warmth.

So the days of living in children's homes came to a close. Terry was old enough to embark upon working for a living. He was still in care, however, and a farm job was found for him. It was a residential job and, strangely, only a stone's throw from Newport.

It was a good life, and he was on extremely good terms with the farmer and his wife, who treated him well. Even after he left there to join the army they sent him letters and gifts. He recalls those days with pleasure.

Terry joined the army for three years. He had become accustomed to institutional life and moving around, so it was small wonder that he became unsettled on the farm and wanted to join up. Also it was no coincidence that by then he was out of care and could make a move of his own choosing. One of the tragedies, though, was that he had no home of his own and consequently had no place to go when he was on leave from the army. He made one or two visits to the last children's home he was at; he really had nowhere else he could go. One of his army friends took pity on him once, and he spent a holiday at his home. They parted shortly afterwards on posting, however. Terry became a very lonely young man. The three years passed by, and it was time for him to leave the army.

The year was 1953. Fourteen years before he had been removed from his home in Newport and had never returned to the town. Now, on his discharge from the army, he went back there. Terry cannot understand why; neither, for that matter, can I. Somehow or other he was drawn to the place.

At first he didn't know where to go because he knew nobody. Then he became curious. This was the town where he had spent the first four years of his life. Perhaps there was something there that would make some impact on him. He wandered the backstreets of Newport looking for clues to his early childhood.

Earlier in the day he had wandered up Stow Hill. At sometime in his life he had found out that it was on this hill that the children's home was situated. (He didn't know then that Dennis had actually passed the home on his last journey up this hill.) But there he was now in Newport's dockland, looking at the great transporter bridge that spans the River Usk. A small light appeared at the back of his mind. He could actually remember crossing this bridge to some playing fields. He wandered on, but there was to be no more enlightenment. Memory eluded him.

These streets were different. Once upon a time the houses had been large and high, but now they seemed small. The streets were narrow, dirty, and dingy. Then Terry stopped and looked at the name of one street. The name was familiar.

Come on, Terry, you remember. Your sister wrote a letter to you a few years ago, and you kept the address from the top of the letter. That's it, search for it. Look in all your pockets, your wallet. Good. You have found it. This is the street. Now the number. The odd numbers are on that side of the street. There it is. Hold it a second, though: they may not be living there now. When we were young we moved house very regularly, and it is quite possible that they have moved on. Well, Terry, brace yourself.

Terry did just that, and knocked on the door. The door opened. Terry looked at the lady facing him, without recognition. She spoke first. 'Are you our Tommy?' Terry told her who he was, and she told him that she was his married sister. He was taken into the house, where he met his mother. It had been a long time since he had last seen her, a lifetime. Strangely enough, the conversation was all small talk. Terry was introduced to his brother-in-law and his young nephew, and later met other members of the family. Not all of them, however, because there were some who had very little or no contact with the family.

Terry lived there for a very short while, and then he moved on. He remained in Newport but went his own way, visiting members of the family on odd occasions. Then Terry met a young lady, the girl he would eventually marry.

It's a strange business, living so close yet being so distant. It is of nobody's choosing; it just happens that way. Fortunately, when we talk to our brothers and sisters now we can use Christian names; when we were with our mother it was a different matter. What could we call her? Neither Terry nor I were able to bring ourselves to call her Mum.

We were brought up in care, and we know what we missed - the everyday, taken-for-granted things: people to call Mum and Dad; being together as a family through pleasure and adversity; watching each other grow up; family photographs ('This is Mum, this is Dad, these are my brothers and sisters'), not photographs of groups in children's homes. We hated categorization. We were just children, and we wanted fun and love. We wanted to grow up as normal kids. We knew what our feelings were towards our parents; it was difficult enough for us to live with these feelings without others trying to attach blame to them.

We wanted the simple things in life. Decent meals in a cosy and welcoming home. Skipping merrily off to school with a few sweets in our pockets. Being treated as kids with a desire to learn, not kids from a problem family to be mocked and humiliated and pushed to the back of the class until refusal to go to school became the order of the day. We wanted to have birthday parties, to invite friends who would come to our house. We longed to be accepted. We knew that our unwashed bodies, our filthy, cast-off clothes made it difficult for others to accept us as people, but we would have liked a little effort to be made.

I am now a happily married man with two fine sons, a nice home and a good, worthwhile job. I still feel from time to time that I am harbouring a guilty secret. My wife has always been aware of my origins, and I told my sons about my early life years ago, but I still worry that friends and colleagues may discover my background for themselves and judge me for it, as I have never been able to talk about it openly. If I write of those experiences now, it is with feeling and in the hope that something I say may help to promote a more caring attitude among those who work with deprived children.

As for Terry, he too is happily married and has two wonderful daughters. His family knows what he has been through because he has told them. He has never spoken to anyone else about the events I have described. Terry has been tortured for years by his memories of the past. Now the position is better. He feels so much more at ease that he has even sought out some of the old friends whom he knew at the children's home to which he was moved after Bank Farm. Although the memories are still very painful at times, he feels much freer.

Neither of us will ever be able to forget the days that are gone or the regrets that linger, but somehow I think that we will both be better able to live with our memories now.

8 Who Goes Free?

Reginald Gough was sent to prison for six years, his wife for six months. This was in 1945, a long time ago. It would seem that they fully deserved the punishment meted out to them. Lord Denham made this statement in the House of Lords: 'It is my view that Mr Gough, who has been sentenced to six years' penal servitude, would be very much better treated if, during the next six years, every quarter, or every six months, he could have ten or sixteen blows with the cat or whatever the implement is called.'

Time has passed, and Mr and Mrs Gough have completed their sentences as far as the law is concerned. I wonder what they must think when they look back to those days. What are their feelings whenever a new case of child brutality hits the newspaper headlines? Are they still prisoners of their own torment? They may be; on the other hand, they may well have put it all behind them.

And what about all the other people? When was it that they were able to escape the dreadful enormity of it all? Although it all took place so long ago, who can yet afford to let Dennis rest in peace? What of the people responsible for the placing and supervision of the children? What of the people who looked after them up to the time of the tragic placement? What of Terry and Fred and the family? How much has been forgotten? Did it all end with the imprisonment of Reginald and Esther Gough? Was the lowering of Dennis's coffin into the grave the final curtain on the drama that culminated in his death? Or did the events leading up to this tragedy have a lasting effect upon the people who in some way or another were involved in it?

I have heard about a foster-mother who for many years was wracked with self-condemnation because she felt that things would have turned out differently if only she had been able to continue looking after the children. It is quite likely that the outcome would have been entirely different had they been removed from her at a later date. She wasn't to know then that this tragedy would occur. I would say to this woman that the boys have never thought about her in any other way than as someone who gave them a great deal of happiness while they were with her.

I was once told that a person who felt that he should have been held responsible for the welfare of the children died some time after the trial of Mr and Mrs Gough. Although the events had nothing to do directly with his death, he died a broken man.

I've seen the parents broken and dispirited. I've seen accusing fingers pointed in their direction. It seems of little consequence that they too have suffered, that after having around them a large family, they were left with almost nothing. My father died the year after Dennis. My mother had to live through it all many times. What excuse could she give? How could she make people see that in the first place it was help she needed rather than condemnation?

I can think of no better way of describing my mother's private hell than to offer an essay I wrote while on the course at Cardiff. It is an essay on poverty, and it doesn't really matter whether or not it is a good one; what really matters is that I was sincere when I wrote it. This was how I saw poverty, how I viewed my mother's part in our story a few years before she died.

Poverty - the State of Being Poor
There was an old woman
Who lived in a shoe.
She had so many children
She didn't know what to do.
She gave them some broth
Without any bread,
Then whipped them all soundly
And put them to bed.

This was, at one time, a popular nursery rhyme. It may well be that years ago this rhyme was repeated to many children as they snuggled into their cots and beds and closed their eyes and then slept the sleep of the innocent and the comfortable. As their eyelids became heavy, the old lady faded from their minds until such time as she would require resurrection to satisfy the child's appetite for nursery rhymes or bedtime stories. In my mind's eye, I still see the picture of the large shoe with children leaning out of the lace-hole windows and sliding down the upper of the shoe.

There is an old woman; she doesn't live in a shoe; she lives in a house. A condemned house, it is true, but a house all the same. She is seventy-four now.

There was a time, a hundred years ago possibly, when she was younger. Time passes and people grow older. She was no exception. As a young lady she was quite pretty. Then she was blinded in one eye. She got married. She had so many children she didn't know what to do. Count them as they arrive. Alive or stillborn, what's the difference? They still add up to thirteen. By some standards maybe, this number is not excessively high. She didn't know what to do. Her husband was, more often than not, out of work. He tried to work, but at that time there wasn't much work to be had. Still they managed somehow. The children were able to beg a few scraps of food here and there. Oh, yes, they lived in a house too. Well, that is an understatement really. They lived in many, many houses. One at a time, of course, dependent often on how long the landlord was willing to tolerate rent arrears. Sometimes longer than others. Talk about no fixed abode.

I don't know if this woman whipped her children soundly and put them to bed. I know that she couldn't afford to give them broth very often. Mind you, she gave them broth sometimes. It's surprising what you can produce from a few bones ('For the dog, mister') and a couple of handfuls of stolen vegetables.

So the years passed until one day, through various channels, the family was separated. By this time the young lady, her childbearing days over, was now an old woman of forty-one years.

She has remained the same throughout the years. She has grown older, of course. She has buried two husbands and has taken a third. They sit now, alone. He is suffering from cancer. She is still blind in one eye and fearful lest she lose the sight in the other eye. Her children have all grown up. They have all left her. To a normal family perhaps seven children, all living, having reached middle age, would be wealth indeed. To this old woman they are not only a reminder other past poverty, but also indicative of her penance. She brought them into the world, then, whatever the reasons, she failed them. She cannot ask their forgiveness. Today she lives in poverty still. Her house is old and dirty. She eats. Not too well, it's true, but she receives handouts from some of her children. She is grateful. She asks nothing from her children. Her children possibly feel that to lavish affection and offers of material comforts on her now would be rubbing salt into the wound. Her penance is real. She suffers, believing she has caused much suffering to her children. Her children are not doing too badly for themselves. They all live in nice houses and have nice jobs. They all eat well and can afford luxuries, not just sugar and margarine now. Some years ago the old woman was offered the chance of a new house. She declined.

Perhaps, though, she has served her time now. Offers of help are being proffered and being accepted more readily. She has given up the fight. She doesn't cry out for help, but one doesn't now feel so patronizing when giving it.

There was an old woman.

There is an old woman.

There may always be an old woman.

This is a story of poverty. It is a true story. The story of a poor, simple woman who, for fifty of her seventy-four years has struggled to live. She doesn't seem to struggle so much now. I tell this story for the simple reason that this is how I understand poverty. I can explain to this woman that within the Welfare State there are certain benefits to be derived. I can tell her that because of her partial blindness she will probably be able to claim extra benefits. Possibly I can alleviate her hardships a little by supplying her with some coal to keep her warm or maybe some food to help her to eke out her money. No matter what I may try to do for this old woman, though, I will never be able to eradicate the condemnations that are within her each time she sees one of her children.

Poverty, according to the dictionary is 'the state of being poor; necessity; meanness; want'. Tell that to the old woman. The words are there for all to see. The heartaches are etched deeply in the lines on her face. Tell her poverty is want. She will probably smile. Only for a while, though. Then she will shake her head and say, 'I know what poverty is.'

It could well be for her a product of a bygone age that overlapped to this day and has left her broken, lonely and old. Lonely, with a family of seven children still living? Yes, lonely. Just another finger of the hand of poverty. Separation for many years, many wanderings, and then somehow, not too far away, is the twilight.

Come, old woman. You've encountered the giants that Pilgrim met. At least, you've had your share of squalor, want and ignorance. Your idleness is with you now as you sit in that dark, dingy room. You can't go very far. You have to sit and think. What do you think, old woman? You can't think of better days; you never had any. Perhaps you think that everything could have been so different. If only times had not been so difficult. Don't be deluded, old woman. You didn't stand a chance. Maybe, old woman, it is that you think that all your seven living children will visit you together. Why not bring their wives or husbands? Perhaps their children too? Perhaps you sit and count on your fingers how many grandchildren you have. You count how many you have seen, and it falls short of the full total. Yes, old woman, you have known for many years what it is to want, and want you still do. Your wants may be different these days. Poverty-stricken old woman. You had almost nothing once upon a time, but now you have even less.

Don't be bitter, old woman. It could have been worse. More of your children could still be living. Don't despair, old woman, you have carried the condemnation for long enough. So now pass the condemnation on to others.

You went wrong, old woman, in that you didn't buy a carpet. Had you done so, we could have swept so much of this under it.

Farewell, old woman, I have to leave you now. I have to leave you with what you have got. I'm sorry I had to use you as an object lesson in poverty, but you have had so much experience.

The last we heard about the old woman who lived in a shoe was when she had put the children to bed. What about you, old woman? What will be the last we hear of you? Will it be that tears will be shed? They won't be yours, old woman. You can't have any left. You don't seem to have much of anything left, do you?

Your children don't thank you for what they are. You had the good grace to do your penance. Perhaps one day they will have the good grace to do theirs.

9 Return to Hope

Nowadays when members of my family meet together we seldom refer to the sad events of the past. If we talk of the old days, it is usually to recall some amusing incident.

I probably think of it more than the others because of my work. I still feel angry about the tauntings and resentful about the way I was treated because of my family's poverty. Even the treats we had as youngsters were given to us because we were poor. As an eight-year-old I remember hating a table-tennis set I was given, knowing that it was a handout, provided out of sympathy for a member of a poor family. If I was invited to a Christmas party, it was not because I was wanted or loved, but because I was a 'needy' child.

I was needy, but I did not need the things I was given or the way they were given. I needed to be lifted out of the conditions in which we lived - not as a punitive measure either for me or for my parents, but as a simple, straightforward act of caring. I needed acceptance as a person, a delinquent maybe, but a real person, an individual who had a right to live a full life.

Where, then, was the hope? As far as I am concerned, it came with the people who were interested in me as a person. They helped me to face up to life as it really was. Sometimes consoling, sometimes sympathizing, sometimes coaxing and cajoling, sometimes catching me by the scruff of the neck and shaking, but always caring, always helping. I was one of the lucky ones. I have known many others who were not as fortunate as myself.

The issues of my childhood are still with us today. We are still concerned about the children who are placed in foster-homes or children's homes because there is no other place available, children who have almost no contact with their social workers, children who often have nobody to champion their cause. I once heard a social worker say that he felt satisfied when he left a boy with us because he knew the child would be cared for. I say, it is no good feeling satisfied. Social workers must *know*. How can they know if they never visit? How easy it is for residential staff merely to feed and clothe the children in their care, to make excuses - overwork, shortages of staff, difficult children - to ignore the real problems and lay the blame elsewhere.

What have we to offer? What can we do for the children who come to us? Sometimes the only thing we have is hope. Over the years I have felt terribly uneasy when I have heard a child being referred to as a 'hopeless case'. It frightens me for two reasons. First, the futility of the job - we are wasting our time if we cannot offer even a glimmer of hope to the kids in our care. If we feel like this about a child, we have given up the will to do something for that child. The second reason why I shudder is because I wonder if this was ever said about me. It is likely - possibly it was said many times. Then someone cared. Sometimes I meet people in child care work who claim that they would consider it to be a good job if it weren't for the kids. I have heard this said in all seriousness.

I would like to tell you two stories about people connected with the child care service. The first is about a lad who had had a very chequered career. The odds were stacked against him from the start. His father was a drunkard, and his mother ran away from home. The boy got into quite a lot of trouble with the police, and one day he was sent to a probation hostel. When his stay at the hostel had been completed, he returned home to his father. Time passed; nothing was heard of the boy for a very long time. Then the warden received a letter from the boy's father. According to the letter, the boy was keeping out of trouble, had got himself a steady job and was working regularly. The father wrote that he wished to thank the warden for the good work he had done for the boy. Then he went on to say this: 'Since A returned home, the newspapers that we had to cover the meal table have now been replaced by a tablecloth, and, do you know what, sir, the grub tastes better.' I have heard the warden tell this story many times, and on each occasion there was a gleam in his eye that told us that he knew he had achieved something for this boy.

The second story concerns a very large family. The home was in an appalling condition, and the mother was inadequate to cope with such a large family in such surroundings. The decision was taken to receive the children into care and to rehouse the parents. The children would be returned to their parents after a suitable settling-in period. However, the children, three boys and one girl, remained in children's homes for a long time. They got older, and one by one they left school and returned home. The two eldest boys returned first. They were both working by this time, and it was thought that they would be of some help in the home. The house had deteriorated somewhat over the years and was now in a dirty state and needed internal redecoration. These two lads took it upon themselves to do something about it and started in their own bedroom. A social worker visited and was asked to have a look at the bedroom. She did so and in her report wrote that the two boys had tried to redecorate a bedroom but hadn't made a very good job of it. Possibly a fact plainly stated, but surely the important thing was that they themselves had attempted to do something about the conditions in which they were living? Surely the quality of the work was of less importance than the fact that the boys had made some effort to make their home a little better than it was? I am not trying to say that one social worker was doing a good job and the other wasn't, but there was certainly a difference of attitude towards, and understanding of, the children concerned.

A long time has passed since the tragic events of Hope Valley. Great strides of progress have been made since that day. Many thousands of children have been helped through their tender childhood, their turbulent years of adolescence and even their early adulthood. Many children have grown up grateful for the help that they have received from Children's Departments all over the country. Much has been done to improve the skills of the people who choose to work with children. A better understanding of children's needs has been pursued. Books by the score have been written to bring to each and every one of us the knowledge that will help us to get to grips with some of the problems that confront us in our work with children. Far more important than this, though, is the need to have a real feeling for the kids who come to us. How easy it is to label these children 'thugs', 'layabouts', 'thick as two short planks', 'useless', 'lazy', 'like his father', 'a waste of time', 'hopeless'. How sad that all is, but how much sadder when the label is made to stick.

How lonely these children are sometimes. How they must lie awake at night and think and cry, and cry and think. How bleak the future must look to them. How guilty most of us are. How often do we look upon something as trivial when it is important to a child?

Some time ago I accompanied a social worker taking a boy to a remand home. Just after our arrival a questionnaire was completed from answers given mainly by the boy. The boy wasn't very bright; when asked his date of birth, he could only give his age and his birthday date, not the year of his birth. The person filling in the form, the deputy superintendent, made a quick calculation and filled in the year of birth as 1958. Now, the boy had told him he was fourteen years of age, so the deputy calculated accordingly. But the fact was that in a couple of months from then the boy would be fifteen. This made his year of birth 1957. I pointed this out to the deputy, but he wasn't particularly interested. He completed the form and seemed satisfied. I had to get angry before he bothered to check. A triviality? Indeed not. Quite a number of my family, including myself, had come up against this problem, and it had caused us quite a lot of anxiety and inconvenience. It was thought at one time that my brother Dennis was backward at his lessons. Nobody knew that he was trying to work at a level two years above his age.

The problem still arises today. I can remember a boy coming to us and stating, after he had been with us for a few months, that he would like to stay at school a further year. He only had a few months left at school, and I decided to have a chat with him about this. I passed the information on to a social worker, who then checked his birth certificate because, according to her file, he was not due to leave school. She came back with the news that he was, in fact, a year younger than he thought. I had to tell the boy, and it was a great shock to him. A short while later I had another boy admitted to the home who gave me a different birth date from the one that appeared on his documents. The lad was fairly intelligent, and he was adamant that the date of birth he had given me was the correct one. In this instance the difference was a matter of days. I thought that I had better telephone to check with the social worker in his home area. She confirmed the date of birth as being that which appeared on his file. I was just about to replace the receiver when I thought that I had better make a double-check. I asked her the source of her information and she replied that she obtained it from his file. I asked her to check with his birth certificate. She did so, and the date this time tallied with the one that the boy had given me. Damn it all, these things are *important*. Certainly they are to a child, and should be to the persons responsible for the well-being of that child. Isolated cases they may be - but so was Bank Farm.

My brother Terry went through his early years moving about from one place to another, receiving some good treatment and some bad from those who looked after him. One day kindness, the next cruelty. He formed no real relationship with anybody. He moved from home to a foster-home, to a children's home, then back to a foster-home and once more to children's homes for about seven years. For him there was no anchorage; he just went where he was told. He grew up and went into the services. He was in a strange new world, and there was nobody he could go to for help, nobody who really knew him, so he just plodded clumsily on. He longed for somewhere to go, somewhere that he could call home, but he had nothing. He knew that an eternity ago he had had a mother and possibly brothers and sisters. Where were they now?

For fourteen years he wandered. At one time he was at least with other members of his family, but now he was alone. He had been alone for a long time now. He wasn't an easy lad to manage, but who would have been, given the circumstances? He wasn't very well-educated either, but this was due to traumatic experiences and the moves of his childhood rather than to his own inability to learn. For all that, somebody could and should have taught him the meaning of the word 'love'. He should have known the significance of the lap, or the hand placed tenderly upon his head. It is small wonder that he didn't cry much during his childhood and youth. There was no recipient for tears. The sadness was his; he couldn't share it.

Throughout his fourteen years of wandering the whereabouts of his family were kept from him and his from them. It must be acknowledged, in all fairness, that his family didn't make much effort to find out where he was. But should that have been necessary? He was a child, a child who had endured a lifetime of suffering in a few short years. Over-dramatization? Not a bit of it. He was not just a statistic; he was a very deprived human being, somebody who needed love and wanted somebody to tell him that he was important. Even his suffering became a problem to the very people that should have been caring for him. The spell of happiness that he had after his harrowing experiences at Bank Farm was curtailed. The reason does not matter. There can be no excuses, no justification. He was not only the product of a problem family; he was also the product of a problem service.

Eventually, Terry found his family, or at least what remained of it. His mother, sisters and brothers welcomed him, it is true, but he had left as a child and returned as a man. The years had taken their toll, and he was still a stranger in their midst. Alone he came, and alone he remained. He carried a burden; nobody was prepared to dispel his confusion. He needed enlightenment; nobody would enlighten. To all others the years of torment were in the past, but to him they were very much part and parcel of his life. He couldn't share his heartbreaks or his sorrow; he carried them alone. Still his family cannot understand his anger; still they cannot understand his very deep and real concern for suffering children.

He bluffed his way through life with a broad grin and a devil-may-care manner. To him he was the odd one out in the family. He thought that it was only he and his two brothers who had been removed from home. Nobody would tell him why. Nobody took him to one side and explained the facts. Perhaps the reticence of his family is understandable. But he was a long time in care not knowing the reasons why. He could have accepted the truth. He asked often enough as he got older, but the only information he could glean from any quarter was that he was in care until he was eighteen. Nothing more, nothing less.

He was thirty-five years old before he knew the true circumstances of his removal from home. Again and again he has lived through the torments and tortures of his previous experiences, but all the time he has lived through them alone. How easy it would have been for one of us to have shared them with him. Perhaps it had to be only when the time was right. As far as he is concerned, there were many people who could have helped him, both inside and outside his family. It didn't really need an expert social worker, just a warm, feeling, understanding human being.

For myself the separation was different. There were some similar aspects, it is true. I too was away from home. The reason for my removal was different. I had brought it upon myself, but had I not done so, I would have been removed in a few short months with the others anyway. I had had my share of beatings. I too was lonely and miserable. I didn't get pushed around so much as my brother, though. Not for me a succession of foster-homes. I only went to three institutions. They were meant to be punitive, but as it turned out they were not nearly as punitive as one of the foster-homes in which my younger brother was placed.

In two of the places I went to my isolation was aggravated by the handling I received. It certainly could have had a lasting effect that would have resulted in my whole life remaining a heap of ruins. Fortunately for me, in the third institution, the Salvation Army hostel, things were different. This was where the difference lay in our two lives. I was lucky enough to meet people who really cared.

At last I was looked upon as a person. I was able to develop. I found people with whom I could discuss the things that I felt important to my whole existence. I could talk freely about my upbringing. I could air my problems, no matter what they were. I could weep without feeling ashamed of my tears. I didn't have far to look for help and guidance. Of course, the people who cared for me knew I was ignorant and self-conscious, but there was no derisive laughter. I was not treated as an outcast. They may sometimes have despaired of me, but still help was forthcoming. I never felt deserted. I couldn't understand my problems; I didn't know why I couldn't sleep at nights, why I felt so very, very lonely at times. Perhaps the people who were dealing with me didn't know either, but they tried to understand. It took me a long time to realize that they looked on me as an equal.

Many ordinary everyday things baffled me, causing me embarrassment on numerous occasions, but I was not ridiculed. I had been when I was younger, but now I was a teenager growing into manhood and was treated with the consideration due to me. It meant a lot of hard work for the people at the hostel. Sometimes I misunderstood their intentions. Because it was a hostel that was religiously biased, I sometimes thought they were only interested in my soul. I discovered that this wasn't the case, and when I spat in their eyes, they merely wiped away the saliva and carried on caring. I almost said that they carried on their work. That would have been a grave injustice. These people had no working lives; rather, they were living works. Sentimentality? Again, no. They were there as people helping people. Time meant nothing. Day or night, if the need was there, so was the caring. Perhaps it was not very professional, but you can take it from me that it was effective.

When I left there to go to lodgings or later into the RAF, their affection and caring concern pursued me, all the time helping me to develop and to appreciate the normal things in life. Even when I was hundreds of miles away from their influence, they cared and did all that they could to help. There was one time when I was going through a difficult patch while stationed with the RAF in Lincolnshire. A young Salvation Army officer was contacted by telephone and that evening, at great inconvenience to himself, travelled sixteen miles through the dark, wintry night to help me through my difficulties.

I was encouraged to take up reading and learning. I had missed a lot of schooling, and although I was of average intelligence, I had been held back because of this. But there were so many simple things I had to learn. I found out that you had a special spoon for soup and that soup was not itself a main meal. I was able to visit people's homes to discover that 'best butter', as I called it, was not used exclusively by 'toffs'. I would have been seventeen or so before I drank tea or coffee from a nice china cup. Up to that age I had never been for a meal in a pleasant cafe or restaurant. These places were for people of a different standing from myself. I was awkward in such surroundings; I was unsure of myself and of the people around me. I learned to accept responsibility. I learned how to live with other people. My days were fraught with obstacles and stumbling blocks, but I learned.

One lesson I was taught was to remember where I had come from so that I could help others who came from similar backgrounds. I am grateful to all the people who were my teachers. I am grateful, in a way, that I was once in care.

I look back now to 1945, to Hope Valley, and I think that there was the place where it all began. Out of torment, terror and tragedy came hope. From that place, for many thousands of children in care, came a new charter. We never want to return there, but surely we never want to forget it either. We must look forward but at the same time remember from whence we came. We look after children; they have a right to live and grow. They have a right to a fair chance in life.

Change is inevitable, but we must never again become so bogged down by problems that the child becomes the last person to be considered. The children we care for have suffered enough already; it should be our responsibility to try to alleviate their suffering. Often they have become sceptical of the adult world because of the double-dealing they associate with it. We must deal honestly with the kids we receive. It is very difficult at times to do so, but in the long run the kids get to feel that we are people to be trusted, and this is the first step towards achieving the aims of our work.

In 1945 many excuses were offered in explanation of the series of events that resulted in Dennis's tragic death. They have a familiar ring today. One excuse was the shortage of staff. How many offices are short-staffed today? We often hear of social workers who are carrying case loads that are far too heavy for them. Another excuse was difficult times; it was, admittedly, wartime. We don't have to be told that we are living in difficult times today as far as social workers are concerned. They are all going through a period of change and upheaval, trying to cope with the problems of providing a satisfactory service when they are often not sure themselves of the direction in which they are heading. An inexperienced officer was filling in for someone else, they claimed in 1945. Have you heard that excuse recently? Then, of course, we come to the placement at the farm. The official explanation was that there were no other vacancies. So anywhere, would do? It still happens today. Children are placed in unsuitable environments, resort to deviant behaviour to signal their un-happiness and are blamed when alternative accommodation has to be found for them.

I have cause to be grateful to the child care service. The pressures are enormous, and confusion is evident in many places, but there is still hope. There must always be hope. We see the children as they come to our doors. Often they are afraid and bemused; their faith in people has been shattered because of the disappointment and rejection they have already experienced. For many of them it is a strange new world they are entering. What can we offer them? We bid them welcome, knowing very well that they would much rather be at home with their own parents. We show them their clean beds, their own flannels and towels. We introduce them to all the wonderful playthings we have. We try to keep them amused. We offer many of them 'another chance'. The social worker pats them on the head as she departs and says, 'Now you be a good boy.'

I believe that we can offer these children a home and hope for the future, so that when they leave us they can be ready to take their place in society and look the world squarely in the face. The trouble is that often when they leave us they are not quite ready to do so, and sometimes they are given very little real support.

Is it still as Terry remembers it? 'I was eighteen and this children's worker came to see me and said, "You are now out of care. Congratulations!"'

10 The Pleasure is Mine

It was my original intention that the previous chapter should be the last word. However, it was suggested to me that I should write something about my work with children, and I do that with pleasure. For all that had gone before, I think that my most enjoyable moments and my most fruitful years were those spent working with children in residential homes. Of course, there were moments of depression. There were times when my wife and I were saddened by the circumstances which resulted in the kids' arrival at our home. But what joy we have shared over the years! Yet there would have been no point in it all if the pleasure had been ours alone. After all, we were working with and for kids; we wanted them to benefit from their stay in our home.

In writing about some of the boys we knew and cared for and some of the experiences we shared, I will suppress names in many cases. But there are three people who have been so closely associated with me in my work that they deserve first mention - and by name. I make no apology for identifying them: they are Gwyn, my wife, and my two sons, Bernard and Philip. To them I say a sincere thank you, not only for all that they have done to help me over the years, but also for the way in which they helped many of the children who were entrusted to our care. I am sure that I have influenced the boys I have worked with to a greater or lesser degree; you can take it from me that no one has influenced them more than my wife and my two sons.

Often we pick up newspapers and magazines and look through the advertisements pages to see what jobs there are vacant in residential work. We read the words: 'This is a joint appointment.'

During our years in residential work all our positions have been joint appointments. We would have had it no other way. The main point is that they were in the truest sense *joint* ventures, involving the whole of the family. Without the involvement of all four members, I really feel that we would have been unable to meet the requirements of the job that we wanted to do.

I know that in residential homes one of the problems facing married staff is the upbringing of their own children. Many fear that their own children will suffer. Often the staff children are not accepted by the children in the home, and all too often the children in the home are treated as 'homes kids' by the staff children. As far as we were concerned, every one of us was part of a community. We all had differing needs and we all sought help from one another. I think, more often than not, this was forthcoming. I remember that when it was convenient to the staffing of our establishment that we should become non-resident, one of the great difficulties that we had to overcome was the fact that our two sons were apart from us for long periods of time. Of course, they were growing up and away from the community, just as the older boys in the home used to. Nevertheless, it was a difficult period because we lost so much of their help. It is significant that the old boys who come back to see us always ask after Bernard and Philip, and that our sons still have in their circle of friends some of the old boys of our home.

Everyone took part in the activities in the home - boys, staff, staff children. Of course, there had to be leadership, and I provided that, but I hope it can never be said that in doing so I let others do all the hard work. I must put on record that I could never have carried out all the work involved in running a home - both the everyday activities and the special events - without the tremendous co-operation that we managed to achieve. The successes belong to all of us.

Over the years we held many functions, always with a purpose. We took part in sports - football, table tennis, cricket. We devised fund-raising schemes, both for our own welfare fund and to help outside organizations (we used to send donations to a homeless families fund). We held fetes, Christmas concerts and bazaars, jumble sales. We entered carnivals and fancy-dress parades and on innumerable occasions helped other organizations to raise money by putting on our own sideshows at their fetes. One year we were asked to appear at no fewer than seven fetes that were held locally, which indicated to me that we were very much part of the community and were accepted as such. Obviously, all these activities were time-consuming and hard work - but all of it was worth while.

So what was the point of it all? What were we trying to achieve? Perhaps a good example of our fund-raising efforts is our Christmas concerts. No boy, member of staff or even outside friend who participated in one of our Christmas concerts is likely to forget it. As a matter of fact, whenever an old boy visits us the conversation invariably turns to our Christmas shows.

Usually these lasted about three hours and were, to all intents and purposes, variety shows. They were always light-hearted and humorous in content and were enjoyed by audience and participants alike. (Two years ago I announced that this would be the last Christmas concert that I felt able to put on. There were tears in the eyes of the audience that evening, and we sang Christmas carols for forty-five minutes after the show should have finished. Since then I have been tempted to produce yet another final Christmas show.) On the face of it, these concerts were put on for the sole purpose of fund raising. In actual fact, although fund raising to buy Christmas extras was very much a part of their function, that wasn't the only reason for the shows.

First, the preparation. For the Christmas concerts this was started during the week that the boys returned from their summer holidays. We would have a Christmas show once every two years. Every other year at this time we would prepare for a forthcoming fete or some other venture. You see, we discovered that on their return to the home after the long summer holiday our boys were very unsettled. Starting a strenuous activity straight away enabled the kids to settle in much more quickly. Consequently, we found that very few of the boys ever absconded.

We tried to show that we could only manage to stage a good concert through hard work, upsets, a great deal of joy, a feeling of needing others and being needed by others. Teamwork was required, and there were certainly no passengers at these times. Everybody made some contribution towards the concert, even if it was only putting things away and tidying up after rehearsals. (It never really came to that because it didn't take long for everybody to be carried away by it all.) We spent many hours working side by side and had a tremendous amount of fun in doing so.

Then the concert itself. The presentation was one way of showing off. We reckoned we had the best group of kids in the country and wanted everybody to know. All the boys, male staff and staff children took part in the actual acting. The ladies, including the domestic staff, designed the costumes, organized the refreshments and made sure that all the kids had their own costumes and props for the show. At the end of it we patted each other on the back and thanked one another.

I could relate many stories about our Christmas concerts, but I will confine myself to one. It concerns a lad I will call Bill and a local school teacher who is also a part-time housefather at our home. Bill was a boy with a lot of problems. He had very poor eyesight and wore spectacles that continually slipped to the end of his nose. He had a speech defect. He had difficulty in walking and trouble with balance, which was aggravated by the fact that he was very fat.

He was so keen to take part in the concert that although he was singing with the Minstrel Troupe, I considered that he could take part in some of the sketches. I gave him parts in three. The first sketch Bill was in was the opening sketch of the show. In this he was a football referee. Bill went on in his referee's kit; he deliberately left his spectacles off and groped his way on to the stage. When he turned his back on the audience and started to sing, he not only brought the house down but also convinced some in the audience that they had been right all along about football referees!

In the second sketch he was brilliant. This time he was a member of an all-women working party. It went like a bomb.

However, it was the third sketch that was the crux of the whole business. Although Bill was so eager to take part, he was rather useless. In rehearsals he kept forgetting his cue or his lines. As soon as he came into the sketch, it tended to fall flat - much to the annoyance of a few of the boys with whom we persevered. Now, in the third sketch we had the young school teacher, Brian, acting the part of a psychiatrist. Bill was supposed to visit him with a problem, and at the end of the sketch Bill was supposed to become very angry with the doctor. It was a complete waste of time. No matter how we chivvied him, he just couldn't do it. Came the day of the full dress rehearsal. As soon as Bill entered, the sketch went flat. Not just that sketch, but everything else he was in too. However, this was the part he had to get just right. I bawled him out at rehearsal, then did another run-through of the sketch, mainly for him. He improved enormously. So we had to leave it there for that evening.

In the show when we came to his third sketch of the evening we kept our fingers crossed. He made his entry, sat through his interview, said his lines and acted his part. He was magnificent. Then it was time for him to be angry. He leapt from his chair and attacked the doctor. Brian was taken completely by surprise and landed on his back with Bill on top of him. He screamed out his punch line, which was a joke. The audience was hysterical, and Bill ran off-stage to thunderous applause and laughter. When Bill got off-stage he met my wife, and he said, 'Oh! Auntie, I've done something terrible.' She asked him what he had done, and the reply he gave was: 'I put my foot right on Uncle Brian's private.' That was over two years ago. A few weeks ago somebody said to me, 'I will never forget the night Bill took part in your show. He was fantastic.' Bill, son, I will never forget either. You were a star for one night.

After the curtain fell there was the clearing up. There was a lot of tidying up to do, particularly when we had Minstrels because a terrific amount of washing was necessary to remove the black from the kids' faces. Then, of course, there was all the cash to be counted. This was usually done after all the tidying up. Normally, we counted up around the kitchen table. Everybody tried to get their hands on the cash. Well, why not? After all, this was part of the harvest of their hard work. (Incidentally, we used to take a collection during the concert. The kids themselves did the collection and used open dishes to gather the money.) It was great to see the kids counting the money and looking at it in a way that showed that they considered it to be money that they had earned - which, of course, it was.

And that reminds me of an incident that occurred one year when we decided to hold a fete to raise some extra cash for our own welfare and amenity fund. The date had been fixed and all the preparations made. The evening before the fete arrived, and we had a meeting to sort out the various jobs that needed doing. George had arrived at our home a few weeks before. He was intelligent, and I gave him a job that I considered he could do quite well. After the meeting he came to see me and explained that he thought I had made a mistake. I had given him a job to do alone. I told him that there was nobody I could spare to work with him and that I believed he could do the job quite well, but if he thought that the work was beyond him, he should change with somebody. He said that he could do the job all right, but wasn't I afraid that he would nick some of the money he would be handling? I asked him what the point would be; it would be his own money that he was stealing. The money earned would be spent on outings and treats for the kids. No money, no outings. He went away quite happy and did a fine job.

After our concerts and fetes we always held a kind of inquest. It was important to get together and laugh over our mistakes and take pleasure in our success. It was important to remind ourselves that our success sprang from the fact that we had all worked hard and we had all worked together - to acknowledge that we had achieved because we had attempted.

Then there were the sporting activities. It would have been too easy to give the kids a ball to kick around or a cricket bat to swing. But that wasn't at all the attitude I took. We had at our disposal the means and facilities to teach our kids that working (and living) with others was important. We played games for hours; often on Sunday afternoons we came in from the field with our limbs aching, afraid to sit down in case we couldn't get up again. We used what we had and gained a great deal from it.

Let me tell you about Frank. For a number of years we entered a six-a-side cricket tournament. We always did remarkably well. I suppose we were bound to really, because the kids believed in themselves. It's surprising how many of our kids felt they could play cricket because they actually donned cricket gear, all the way down to their boots. I have heard other staff from other homes say, 'Now they look like cricketers.' They looked good; they felt good; and they played with pride. Of course, we practised for hours. It didn't really matter what the activity was, we reasoned that we would never be successful if we didn't work at it. Life itself doesn't come that easy.

That year we were just starting to think about the cricket season when Frank arrived on the scene. Frank couldn't play cricket and was afraid of a cricket ball. I was at an advantage because I couldn't play cricket either, and although I wasn't afraid of a cricket ball, I certainly wasn't over fond of it. But I was there with the rest, taking the kids at cricket practice.

Frank had a terrible traumatic period of settling in, and we were all very worried about him. Gradually, he began to take an interest in his surroundings and used to accompany us to cricket practice. As time went on, he became quite enthusiastic; eventually, because of his enthusiasm, he was picked for the cricket squad. Then, much to his amazement, he made the final eight - six players and two substitutes. But his pleasure and pride quickly gave way to apprehension; he asked me if I would take him out of the team because he was afraid of letting the other lads down. I told him that if he really didn't want to play, naturally I would agree to exclude him. I also told him that his very request proved to me that the last thing he would do would be to let the others down.

So he played. He played in all the matches, and we eventually reached the final. Along with the rest, he played his part well, and at the end of the tournament we emerged the winners. In the tournament the winners and losers each received a trophy and the winning team a magnificent cup. The cup is returned after one year but the medals become the players' property. The boys trooped along to the pavilion to receive their trophies. Frank received his, then slumped into a chair on his own. I walked over to him, and he said, 'I want to cry, Uncle.' I replied, 'If you want to cry, Frank, then you cry, and I will probably cry with you.' Then he said, 'But, you see, Uncle, this is the first time I have ever won anything in my life.'

We went home and there was great jubilation in the house. The boys wanted to put their individual trophies around the cup - all except Frank. He refused to allow his trophy to be taken from his hands. The other kids complained, and I went over to Frank to explain to him that even celebrating had to be a team effort. We shared each other's tears and joys. He relented.

Over the years we won many tournaments, and the joy was always real. I never really got used to it because each year there was a different Frank.

Another event in which we participated for a few years was the World Hoop Championship. This was a great day out for the boys. (Unfortunately, one of our boys went into the dressing-rooms one year and was caught searching through the pockets. Whether or not it is coincidental I don't know, but the race has not been held since.) The race was held at a speedway track during an interval between races. The crowd was usually in the region of 7000. They were unaware that most of the boys participating came from children's homes. It was held once a year. We took part for three years running and were undefeated. In fact, we entered twelve boys each year, and our worst effort was when we had only ten in the first twelve home! I was well aware that, although billed as a world championship, it was merely an interval gimmick. There was nothing at stake. But it was important. If we chose to enter, then we must do the best we could. So we spent hours practising.

We had a football field, and I marked out on it a track with the same dimensions as the speedway track. None of the kids could bowl a hoop when we first started training, but they became quite proficient as time went on. Again, in this sport we had a ready-made activity which provoked a great deal of merriment and helped the boys not only to try to be better than the rest, but also to help the others. There was one boy (I shall call him Joe) who, by some fluke, managed to chalk up one of the twelve best times. We were restricted to twelve entries, so we had to have a series of eliminators. We took the twelve boys with the best times. On one run Joe made a very fast time, but for the remainder he was all over the place. He was always avoided at the starts because he created havoc. When it was discovered that he was in the race the other eleven said, 'Don't stand next to me.' Joe replied, without batting an eyelid, 'Don't worry. I'll help you lot. I'll stand among the opposition.' And he did. A silly game really, I suppose, but what fun we had on those days.

Football took up a lot of our time. We competed in eleven-a-side league matches and six-a-side tournament matches. (It is worth mentioning that although only a few boys were involved directly in the tournaments, we considered that we were all taking part - in the encouragement, in the training, in the making of banners and rattles. We all shared the setbacks and successes.) There are dozens of stories I could tell, but I will restrict myself to one, which concerns a boy named Jim. Jim didn't particularly like football. He thoroughly enjoyed a kickabout, but when it came to the rough and tumble of real matches, he wasn't very keen. He was quite skilful, a natural left-winger. We were beginning training for a six-a-side tournament, but Jim opted out at the start because he said he had hurt his ankle. Then he became quite enthusiastic until the time came for team selection. He was one of the eight chosen, and he was thrilled to bits. The evening before the tournament we had a warm-up match against another team. Jim informed me that his ankle was playing up a bit, and, sure enough, he was limping. It seemed that he would not be in the right frame of mind to play the next day. However, he got caught up in the fever, and he was quite happy to play. During the day he took quite a bit of stick. We reached the final, and it was decided that Jim would play in it. Right at the start he took a knock. It looked as if he would give in, but he got to his feet and played throughout the match. We won handsomely, and we were all over the moon as the final whistle sounded. As soon as the match was over, Jim ran across to me and burst into tears. I was close to tears myself.

Jim left us, and a long time later I met his mother in his home town. She seemed pleased to see me, and when I asked her how Jim was getting on, she took me aback with her answer. She said, 'You and your bloody football. Jim is out every evening at his local football club. Nothing will stop him going there.' She seemed to be quite angry, then she said, with a gleam in her eye, 'Seriously though, he is mad about playing football and is always going to the club, so we have absolutely no worry about him getting into trouble.' Good on you, Jim.

During the winter evenings we obviously had to take up indoor activities. We played all kinds of games. One group of boys was keen on darts, so on many evenings we put in a couple of hours' practice. Fred was quite interested and could throw a fair dart.

Came the summer, and we put the darts away. Then we took the boys to a holiday camp for a two-week holiday. There were various tournaments going on at the holiday camp, and a darts tournament was among them. Our kids entered all the tournaments and did really well. I entered the darts tournament, along with quite a number of the boys as well as other campers. All the lads got knocked out in the early rounds except Fred. He was doing very well and was quite excited. I too was doing well and, after looking around at the opposition, felt that I was in with a good chance of winning a cup for the first time in my life. I arrived at the final quite comfortably and waited for the other semi-final to take place between Fred and a camper. Fred's opponent finally decided that he would have to withdraw from the tournament. It was a pity, because I felt that I could have beaten him fairly easily. This meant that Fred was through to the final and had to play me. I had one hand on the cup. We played the final, and he thrashed me out of sight. There were some who thought I might have given him the match; but, as I explained later, in the first place I wouldn't have done this because it would have been a hollow victory for Fred, and in the second, I would never have allowed him to beat me so convincingly had I been able to avoid it. Fred claimed that he didn't want the cup anyway; but when I spoke to his mother some time later, she told me that the cup had pride of place on the mantelpiece.

Of course, running a children's home isn't all fun and games. I want now to describe the way in which I worked with the children in my care and the principles I tried to teach my students during the time I trained young people for residential work.

First, a little about the daily routine in our home during the years I was in charge. Not that I particularly liked routines or regular patterns. One example will show what I mean. One evening a boy came in from school and said, 'Ah, Wednesday evening - fish and chips!' I said to myself: we mustn't have this - we're getting in a rut. It was only the case one meal a week; usually boys would come in and say, 'What's for tea?', the most natural thing in the world. But in children's homes there's often a tendency to fall into unnecessary routines: 'It's Tuesday night. We've got sausages and mash.'

In the mornings we did have a routine. A member of staff called the boys at a certain time every morning, and breakfast was always to time. It was the one meal staff did not eat with the boys. I can justify that, though it does sound rather regimented and institutional. (The terrible thing about residential work is that we can justify most things, even though they may be wrong.) I would be in the office, checking through the diary, getting the dinner money ready and so on. Then the boys would be on their way to school. We had no children at home for dinners; they started coming in again between half-past three and about a quarter to five. That was it as far as the routine went. After that, anything could happen.

When I first went to the home there was a semi-circle of chairs around the television set. In those days kids didn't switch on television sets; the sets were switched on for them. When I visited the home before I took over I used to say, 'Isn't it quiet here? Where are the kids?', and the housefather replied, 'Oh, the third member of staff's got them' - meaning the television set. We didn't really have television after I came. If we had switched the television on immediately after tea and switched it off late at night, nothing would have been done during the evening. I thought there was a lot to be done. I felt that the boys (and particularly the ones labelled 'antisocial') came to our place to get the idea of working and living with others. We couldn't do this around the television set. It was terribly important for them to learn to depend on one another.

I used to say to the boys that I was a bit of a cheat because they were doing the job and I was getting the pay. When I left the home I spoke to each of the boys individually. There was one who had been in a reception centre for five weeks, and during that time he had run away nineteen times. He'd never run away from our place. On my last day I asked him why. He said, 'There's no point, is there?' I said, 'Do you mean to tell me you never thought of running away?' He replied, 'No, that's where you're wrong. I have thought about running away - that's the difference. I have thought about it.' Then he went on to say:

> I remember you telling us, 'It's the kids who do the work.' And you went on to say that you hoped I would reach the position where kids would come to me, thoroughly fed up, wanting to run away and wanting me to go with them, and I'd say to them that I couldn't see the point of it. And that's exactly what happened to me. The first few days here I said, 'I'm going to do a bunk,' and one of the kids said, 'No point. If there was a point, I'd go with you.' So he was doing your job.

When the boys came home from school the usual meeting place was the kitchen. We used certain things as barometers of how they were feeling. If a boy who usually came to join us in the kitchen didn't come one day, we'd try to find out why. If a boy who never came into the kitchen did come one day, we asked ourselves, was it because he was settling in? Another barometer was names. I know there are people today who don't like the use of the names 'Uncle' and 'Auntie' in children's homes. I'm not going to say whether I like them or dislike them, but for me they are barometers. Kids called me 'sir'; they called me 'Mr O'Neill'; they called me 'Uncle

Tom'; or they called me 'bastard' behind my back. They always called me something, and the name they chose was indicative of how things were going. I remember a boy calling me 'Uncle Tom' once, blushing to the roots of his hair and saying, 'God, I never thought I'd call you that.' But he admitted then that we got on much better together. I was authority to him up to that time, and then the name slipped out. I think it could have come out a lot earlier, but he had fought it; he wasn't going to bend, to admit we meant something to him, until he used that name.

We never kicked boys out of the kitchen. If boys wanted to help, we let them help. There were chores to be done. I explained to the boys why they had to be done, and there was a terrific feeling of caring for the place. We were living in it, after all, staff as well as children, and we wanted it to be nice; we wanted good facilities.

The highlight of any day in our house was tea. It was unpredictable; we didn't know what was going to happen at tea time. The longest meal we ever had lasted from about a quarter to five until ten to ten. There were jobs to be done, of course, and I was often accused of talking till the cows came home, but on this occasion the people who were waiting to do the washing up came in, sat down and joined in because of the feeling that there was. A boy who had often threatened other kids with what his rich relatives would do to them suddenly said, 'What the hell are you on about? You don't know what it's like to be poor.' And not just that. He said to all the others, 'I've been a liar all these months,' standing up and acknowledging it; and he turned to me: 'Come on, Tom O'Neill, you tell me what it's like to be in care. I'm not here through choice.' On that evening when we finished talking, even though it was late, the kids immediately got up, cleared the tables and washed up because it had been so important to them.

After tea there would be evening activities - table tennis, snooker, games. Often, if it was school holidays, I would take the kids out to the beach and run around on the sand even till midnight. We had a good lie-in the next morning, especially if it was Sunday morning, as we had no cleaners coming in.

Funnily enough, I never really liked the beach. After we left the home my wife said to me one day, 'Let's go down the beach.' I said, 'Oh no, I don't want to go there. I don't like the beach. I hate it really.' She said, 'Oh, come on, you've been going to the beach for years.' And I replied, 'Yes, but I don't like it. I can't stand sand in food, and I certainly don't like swimming in the sea.' But for fifteen or sixteen years I had spent days and days on the beach, and she couldn't believe that; she'd never realized. I'd enjoyed it up to a point, but only through being with the boys.

Another reason why I had gone to the beach was that I had to be with them. In those days there was a regulation about it, and without me there they couldn't have gone at all. (I happened to be the only member of staff who could swim.) I was a stickler for rules like that. Boys used to say to me, 'Can we go in the sea?' and I'd reply, 'No, the red flag's flying.' Sometimes we'd be near a group of boys from another home who were allowed in the sea, and my children found that hard. I explained, 'We're playing by the rules. All the time we're playing by the rules.' It would have been easier to say, 'All right, but don't go out too far,' but that wasn't the point. If we hoped to teach children to be honest and straight, we had to set an example.

If we wanted to get into a theatre half-price, I always asked the permission of the management, explaining we were short of money. It would have been easy to say 'Ten halves,' but the danger was the boys would notice that I was talking about honesty and yet was quite prepared to cheat. Also, it would have been insulting to them to suggest that they could get away with looking younger than they were.

Honesty was one of the principles that I felt very strongly about in residential care. Children would come to us labelled 'anti-social' and 'dishonest'. They were supposed to be the cheats, but very often they had been cheated - especially the ones classed as delinquents. They had been cheated by magistrates; they had been cheated by social workers; they had been cheated by parents. If parents split up, if one parent left the home, if both abandoned the child, that child felt cheated. They weren't being dealt with fairly.

Social workers would often say, 'You'll only be away from home for a few months.' But if a child was, say, eleven years old, there was a very strong possibility that he would remain in residential care until he was sixteen years old. It was really a question of years; yet the child was told it would be months. Magistrates would often say, 'You'll be away for a time, and then we'll see how it goes. . . .' But it didn't work out like that. So the children felt cheated; they *were* cheated.

When a child came into my home I would say, 'Look, whatever has gone on up to now is finished with. This is a new beginning. From now on you're going to be trusted. You are going to be treated with the respect you deserve.' Even with my own strong feelings about honesty, however, I had to guard against falling into the old trap of hypocrisy. A boy might come into the home at three in the afternoon, having been in court since ten that morning. I would ask, 'Are you hungry?' He would say, 'Yes.' And I would be tempted to say, 'Would you like a snack and then wait for the others to come home for a main meal? Otherwise I'll have to fetch the keys to the larder. . . .' And I'd just finished telling him that he was going to be trusted! One minute we claim that the past is forgotten; the next minute we put our faith in them *only up to a point.*

I remember my wife on one occasion asking a boy to run upstairs to the flat, to go to the box in the bedroom and to get some money for the insurance man. I thought: 'Oh God, no, not him!' I had to examine my own reaction very carefully. I don't believe we ever lost a penny by trusting children.

I think that my principles did communicate themselves to the children, and one way I gauged this was by the reactions of my own children. One of my sons in particular seemed to understand very well what I was trying to do. A couple of stories will illustrate this. I was away on the course at Cardiff while my son was taking his A-levels. He was having a very rough time and wanted to talk to someone. He said to my wife, "When Dad comes home at the weekend, I'll talk with him,' and she said, 'He'll be pretty tired.' My son said, 'Well, there's one thing about Dad, it doesn't matter how far into the night, Dad will always find time.'

But there was one occasion when I proved myself unworthy of this accolade. I was still on the course at Cardiff and had planned to have a very quiet weekend at home. I had been seeing a lot of Terry at that time and felt emotionally drained. When I went home one of the old boys phoned me and said that he would like to come and talk to me because his marriage was on the rocks. I said, 'Well, if you don't mind, this weekend I'd like to be free.' He accepted that, and I put the phone down. I felt I'd done the right thing. Because I was away from my family - and over the years I had spent less time with my family than on my work - I thought they should come first now. But my son, who had never sworn at me before, turned on me and said, 'You rotten sod. What's the matter with you? What's this course done to you? Is your head getting that big? This is the first time I can ever remember you turning down a kid who needed your help.' That made me realize just how much they understood - and shared in - the way I worked and how much they wanted me to stay true to it.

One other example will illustrate the part that my children played in the way the home ran. I punished a boy once, and my son, who was eleven years old at the time, knocked at the office door, asking to see me. People only approached me like that if they wanted to see me in an official capacity; if he had wanted to have a chat or to ask for something, he could just have walked in - the door was open anyway. He said, 'You'll probably tell me to mind my own business, but I feel there's something I should tell you.' I said, 'Well, sit down then,' because I felt this was outside the father-and-son relationship. I was the superintendent to him at that moment. I said, 'Okay, what's on your mind?' He said, 'You punished X today.' And I replied, 'Well, you are right, Phil - I would say that's not really your business.' He said, 'Okay, but I think I'd better warn you. If you knew what I know about that boy, you wouldn't have punished him in that way.' I asked, 'Well, what do you know?' He replied, 'Oh no, I was told by him in confidence.' I must have looked across at the filing cabinet because he went on, 'And you won't find it in his file either.' He wouldn't say any more, so I said, 'Well, I'm afraid that there's nothing I can do about it.' But when he left the office I gave the matter a lot of thought. I managed to get hold of the boy later, before the punishment came into effect, and said to him, 'I was so annoyed at the time that I didn't take into account the whole of your behaviour over the last few months, so I'm going to let you off.' Really, I was letting myself off.

Years after this, when I was on the course at Cardiff, we were talking about the old boys, and this boy's name cropped up. I said, 'Ah, Phil, by the way, tell me what it was that you knew about him.' and Phil's answer was: 'It was a confidence then, and it's a confidence now.'

Sometimes the boys in the home would use my children to communicate important feelings to me. One of the boys always got into trouble just before the start of a holiday. It was my son who pointed out to me that he didn't want to go home. Obviously, the boy himself hadn't been able to tell me, but he had told my son. My son had said, 'Well, you tell my father,' and he'd replied, 'I don't like to. It's a very sensitive subject. Could you break the ice?' So there were things they found easier to discuss with my sons than with me. (In this case, in fact, the problem was that the boy's father had been interfering with him during the holidays.)

When I left the children's home I went into teaching at a preliminary residential course nearby, mainly with students who had come straight from school and were often only sixteen or seventeen years of age. Quite a few of my students had been fostered themselves, and I was able to get across to them how they could turn to advantage the fact that they had had experiences similar to those of the children they were caring for.

When I visited students in placements during their course I used to watch for the attitudes of the staff towards the student in their establishment. I couldn't stand a patronizing attitude towards any worker in residential care - cook, gardener or student. It greatly pleased me when students were shown consideration and included in what was discussed; it angered me when no thought or concern was shown them or when they were excluded.

Sometimes what they saw in residential work upset students - unfairness, for instance, and arbitrary rules. I encouraged them to remember those feelings and to recall them when they had responsibility for caring for children. What was wrong for them then would be wrong when they were promoted.

Many students, when they had finished the course, weren't ready for residential work, especially not work with children. They had great potential, but it could have been destroyed in the first year in a job if they had had bad experiences. So it was important for me to get across to them (and to their parents) that any job they might do immediately after the course would help them be more effective residential workers. It was especially difficult for parents to understand this. (My own son got a degree and then worked on the buses. It was experience, and I'm sure it made him a better teacher later.) What I had to say to the parents was that whether my students were good residential workers was secondary; what mattered was whether we had helped them become better people. If they were better people, I believed they would be better nurses, child care officers and so on. If my ex-students worked in Woolworth's or drove vans or whatever after they left the course, *when they were ready to do so* they would use what they had gained from the course. They would use it by going into residential work, or as foster-parents, or in the way they brought up their own children. And this was what really mattered. Even if they never did residential work, being better parents was a kind of preventive work - after all, if all parents were successful, there would be no need for residential work.

But it used to thrill me when, often several years after they left the course, ex-students I had last seen working in shops or offices rang me to say that they had got jobs with children. They weren't going into residential work just because they had been on a course. In fact, the course had taught them that they *weren't* ready to work with children straight away. Only when they felt ready had they chosen to go into the work.

In my own case, I wasn't ready to do the work until I had

experienced love, reliability and honesty - which did not happen until I was seventeen years old. Had I not had the experience of being cared for, I am convinced that I would have been unable to care for others. I wouldn't have known what it was to give care unless I had received it. I had been on the receiving end of dishonesty, and although I had been dishonest myself, I had also been cheated in many ways. Suddenly at seventeen I was told that my past was forgotten, and I was shown what trust and forgiveness really meant. When I let people down they didn't just say, 'Oh, we knew this would happen. We hoped it wouldn't, but we really knew it would.' They went on caring and hoping for better things. The idea that I always tried to get across to my students was hope. Each of them might be the one person, for the first time in a child's life, who recognized a hopeful spark and in turn gave hope.

That was why I emphasized the importance of qualities like honesty, reliability, punctuality. If a student was late for a lecture and apologized, I would say, 'That's all right, but I'm glad I wasn't a child in care waiting for you.' After all, I had experienced that kind of disappointment myself.

The sad thing is that some bits that I and others like me missed in childhood can never be put back again. My own sons have in turn missed out because of that. They were good at making things with their hands; but I never showed them how. That was because my father never showed me how. I wonder if they will be able to show their children?

On the other hand, I believe that my sons have learned a great deal from my life experience. It is not an easy thing to acknowledge to your children the facts of a doubtful background and upbringing. Both my sons accepted them with great sensitivity. I am convinced that the way in which they live and their attitude towards people less fortunate than themselves are due in part to their awareness of my own childhood and youth.

I would like to finish with a handful of stories, some of the many that we could tell about the boys we have known over the years. These are success stories, which makes them easy to write about.

There have been failures too; they have made us aware of our need to care for and about the kids even after they have left us. We get letters from boys who have become successful soldiers, bank clerks, labourers, laboratory assistants, totters, firemen - *people*. They have learned to live with what they are and what they have.

It wasn't long ago that my wife and I were both feeling rather low. We both felt that the years in residential work had taken their toll, and we had had enough. Then, within the space of a week, we received two telephone calls and three letters. They were all from boys whom we had had with us many years before and were all in very much the same vein. They thanked us for the effort we had put into our work with kids. They were glad of the experience of being in care because although they felt that they had missed out on many things, they felt that their time in residential care had helped them to go on to live a worthwhile life. Clearly, these boys and others like them looked upon us as friends; and we looked upon them in the same way.

One evening I was sitting at home with my wife when the doorbell rang. Our visitors were a young man of thirty, his wife and his daughter. We had last seen the young man about twelve years before, three years after he had left our home. We had watched him grow up and leave us, and we knew that he would do well for himself. He came back. He thanked us for what we had done for him. He was proud to introduce his family to us.

Another boy had returned to see us some months before. What he had to say absolutely staggered us. He told us that the reason he was doing so well was *because* he was brought up in care. He was quite serious about this and explained that when he saw some of his friends unsettled or struggling he would tell them that their real problem was the fact that they were brought up in a normal home. He maintained that the happiest years of his life were those spent in a children's home because he was well-fed and well-clothed, had plenty of recreational facilities and companionship and, most important, felt that the people looking after him really cared. He remarked that children brought up in their own homes, by their own parents, often had nobody to guide them, whereas he always felt that the people looking after him had always found time to help him through his difficulties. I cannot say that I can agree with him completely, but that was the way he felt about things, and we must be grateful that he is now a fairly well-adjusted young man.

What a thrill it is when, after a tiring day, late in the evening, a prosperous business man arrives with his wife and announces that he would like to take us out for an evening meal. Regretfully, we tell them that we cannot leave the place because we are the only people working that evening. When they leave he hands his card to us and tells us to telephone when it is convenient for us to spend an evening with them. I remember him well as a cheeky little boy who was not exactly easy to handle.

Chris is now a fireman. I know that he is a good one because he never did anything by half measures. He stayed with us for a number of years and developed into a great chap. Once upon a time he wanted to work in a children's home, and although I would have been more than willing to have him on my staff, it was against the policy at that time to have persons who had been in care themselves working with children. (I'm not quite sure how I managed to slip in.)

Anyway, Chris left us to go into lodgings locally. He started his working life and would often come in to tell us how he was getting along. Then he met a young lady and started going out with her regularly. He often brought her to our home. I remember one Christmas time that in spite of an acute staff shortage, I decided to put on a Christmas concert. Chris came to the rescue by roping in his girl friend and a young married couple to help us with our Christmas show. He also induced the manager of the large grocer's shop where he worked to supply a very valuable raffle prize.

One day Chris and his girl friend arrived and said they would like to have a chat with my wife and myself if it was possible. They told us that they had fixed the date of their wedding, and Chris asked us if we would act as his mum and dad at the wedding. If anybody had walked in on us at that time and heard my answer, he would have thought me an extremely odd person. I said: 'What a crafty way to ask for a wedding present.' Chris knew exactly the way in which I meant it. A good laugh is often a good way to disguise the lump in the throat. We told them that we would be thrilled to do so. Later on in the evening I gave them a lift home. After we had dropped his girl friend out at her house Chris said that he hoped that I didn't mind his making such a request. I told him that if I had thought he wanted to ask us but didn't like to for any reason whatsoever, I would have felt hurt.

Well, they got married and we were treated as his family at the wedding and reception. We still saw them from time to time. One day Chris and his wife came to see us, and as soon as he saw my wife he said to her in the most natural way, 'Congratulations, Auntie. You are going to become a grandmother.' He kissed her, and I knew at that moment that we were far more to them than just a superintendent and a matron.

I have asked Chris to call us by our Christian names rather than 'Auntie' and 'Uncle', but he still prefers to call us that. To him they are terms of affection. How great it is to have so many 'special friends'. Chris and Jean are very much a part of our family. Shades of Tom O'Neill in Reading.

To those folk who are so often moaning that the kids of today are so much worse than they used to be, I say: 'I wish you knew Ted and his wife, Jane.' When we arrived at the children's home Ted was twelve years old, was 5 foot 6 inches tall and was still wearing *short trousers*. He didn't wear them for long after our arrival.

He was one of those kids whom Children's Departments seemed to send to children's homes to ensure that the residential staff earned their pay. He absconded, he stole, he bullied, he truanted and he made life generally difficult for all. I remember that after I had been at the home for about six months I was asked how Ted was getting along. I replied that he was doing fine and hadn't stolen anything for over a week. I got a peculiar look and was asked whether I thought that was progress. I said that indeed I did. If a lad like this had been in the habit of stealing daily, then surely he was making progress if he managed to go for any length of time without stealing? But it is true that no matter what action we took, Ted showed little response. While he was with us he made several court appearances, and he seemed destined to spend most of his life in institutions of one kind or another.

There are some incidents concerning Ted which spring to mind quite easily. When he was about fourteen a family man approached me with a view to having Ted to stay with them for weekends. I was rather concerned because I felt strongly that Ted needed somebody who would accept a lot of deviant behaviour without rejecting him. After a long discussion it was agreed that Ted would benefit by going to their home for weekends, and I was given the assurance that the couple would persevere with him. They would not reject him out of hand if he caused trouble; if there were problems, they would discuss any action with me. After a short while some petty pilfering was brought to my notice, but Ted was allowed to continue with his weekends. Then the family could accept it no longer.

It so happened that our housefather welcomed the man when he came to discuss Ted, and as I approached the office, I heard the housefather saying, 'Of all the boys I have known in children's work I would consider that Ted is the one boy for whom there is no hope.' I walked into the office and said to the housefather, 'John, if you feel that way, I suggest you go and pack your bags and get out of this work. Look at some of the kids we get. If we take away hope, we have nothing left. Our work then becomes a complete waste of time.'

Ted left us for a short while and went into a foster-home, but things didn't turn out too well and, at his own request, he returned to us. He stayed with us after he left school and started work. He seemed to be holding his job down well, and then one day I had a visit from the police. It appeared that one of the men at work had lost a sum of money; because Ted hadn't turned up for work that day, they thought that they had better check. I told them that Ted was at work, but they assured me that he wasn't. Ted did not come in at his usual time, and the evening turned into night. At a quarter to one in the morning he arrived. I asked him where he had been. He told me that a lorry had broken down in the wilds, and he was unable to contact me. Eventually, the driver was able to get some help, but they had had a very slow drive home. I cooked him a meal and listened sympathetically to his tale of woe. He even produced a map on which places were marked where, he said, they had been making deliveries. I took it all in. Then I suggested that it was time for bed. It was now about half-past two. As he was half-way up the stairs, I called him back and said I would like to see him in the office. I told him what I really knew about the day's events. We had a very long talk and then went to bed. When I went to call him just after six he had departed.

(Many years later we discussed the events of that night. Ted said that he considered I had played a dirty trick on him by pretending to believe him, while all the time I knew the truth. Then he really struck home. He said that he didn't mind that aspect of it and, looking back, could see the funny side. What had wounded him was that when we had gone into the office and I was talking to him, I apparently said, 'I have had enough. There is nothing more I can do for you. I have finished.' I cannot remember these words, but I must have said them because Ted said, 'At that moment I felt I had lost everything.' That was the reason he ran away, not because he was afraid of a prosecution.)

This time Ted was away from us for a few weeks. Eventually, he was picked up. It turned out that he had quite a number of charges against him. He made his court appearance and the magistrates decided that they would send him to a detention centre, but only if I agreed to have him back with us on his release. He was seventeen at this time. He went to the detention centre and then returned to us.

One evening when I was off-duty Ted went out and had a few drinks. He came in very late at night and had a fight with the housefather. In the morning he was not in his bed, and he never returned to the home except for a visit. A few days after he absconded I took the boys to a carnival. Ted was now in lodgings locally, and as I was walking along the street, I was astonished to see him pass me by. I called after him. He turned around and came back to me. I gave him the biggest rocket I have ever given anyone. I told him that if he ever passed me by on the street again, I would kick him all over town. I told him that he could do what he liked - he could even spit in my eye - but he was never, ever to ignore me. He looked sheepish; he coloured up a little; but he only said three words: 'Thanks, Uncle Tom.'

Ted went to the Midlands to live and work, and we lost touch with him completely. I heard one day that a former housefather visiting a Borstal institution saw him there and spoke to him. However, we never heard anything from Ted himself.

One day we received a telephone call from Ted, who asked if he could come to see us. Of course, we were delighted to welcome him. On the day in question he arrived with a lady - his wife we were surprised to discover. After the usual pleasantries and reminiscences, they asked if it was possible for them to have a chat with me. It was one of those good days when we were able to find a quiet corner and have a real talk.

Ted said that before he married Jane he had told her every thing about himself. Apparently, he had also told her a great deal about me. He explained that I was constantly telling kids to get into a position from which they could look the world squarely in the face, and then they would be able to do the things they wanted to.

It turned out that after they had been married for a while Ted decided that he would like to start a completely new life and to join the forces. He talked it over with Jane for a long time, and eventually they both decided that it might be a good step to take. So off Ted went to a recruiting office and started to fill in the necessary forms. Then he came to a question relating to prosecutions. At first he thought of telling lies, then he considered that there would be no point in trying to start afresh if the starting-point was going to be deceit. So he filled in all the details. The result was that he was turned down. He was furious. He went home and told Jane that I was a liar, that he would never be allowed to be any different. He told her that I was wrong when I said that he and others like him would be allowed to live down the past.

Jane kept cool and explained that nobody had ever told him that these things would be handed to him on a plate, but rather that if something was worth reaching for, then we sometimes had to stretch a bit. So, after some discussion, they decided that they would approach their local Member of Parliament. The outcome was that Ted should allow a period of time to elapse and then apply again. This was agreed by all parties.

I wish I could recapture for you adequately the conversation as it was going on. To say that it thrilled me would be an understatement. At this point I felt that all that had gone before, the heartbreaks, the frustrations, the disappointments, had all been well worth while. *This* was our 'hopeless case'!

Ted and his lovely wife left us that day and some months later telephoned to say they would like to come and see us again. The day arrived and the doorbell rang. When I answered the door Jane stood well in the background. There stood Ted, resplendent in his uniform. Ted had arrived.

And then there was the phone call from John a short while ago to say that he would like to make a donation for Christmas extras for the kids. When I said, 'That's very kind of you, John,' his reply was: 'Not at all. I had so much from the home while I was there I thought it was about time I put something back in.' I hope we gave you the important things, John.

These are all kids who have done reasonably well. There were others, God knows. We are well aware of this; but although there have been disappointments, they all gave us a great deal of happiness. They were kids and consequently couldn't respond as robots, at the touch of a button, but then we wouldn't have wanted it that way. Many young men and women have said that they have been pleased to have met me. In all sincerity, the pleasure has been mine.

To you all, whether you have been in care, or are still in care, or are working with children in care, I say this: remember that there is *always* hope.

Epilogue

It might be fitting to end this book with a story that seems to sum it up. A Salvation Army officer was retiring, and a ceremony was held to mark the occasion. To his surprise, as a present to show the esteem in which he was held, he was given a plant pot filled with earth. 'What is it?' he asked the presenter, who replied, 'Sir, it's not what it is, but what it might become.'

Index